AMERICAN SOUTHWEST

PLACES AND HISTORY

STEWART, TABORI & CHANG
NEW YORK

Text
Marcella Colombo

Editing Supervision
Valeria Manferto De Fabianis
Laura Accomazzo

Art Director
Patrizia Balocco

Graphic Design
Anna Galliani
Clara Zanotti

Translation
Studio Traduzioni Vecchia

1 *Signs of civilization in Canyonlands National Park.*

2–7 *Two symbols of the American Southwest: in the foreground, an old stagecoach still well-preserved, and in the background, one of the 1,500 arches in Arches National Park.*

3–6 *The Bryce Canyon amphitheater covered with a soft cloak of snow. According to an Indian legend, animals capable of taking on human form once lived in this place. These extraordinary evil beings irritated the gods, who punished them by changing them into rocks.*

Copyright © 1998 by White Star S.r.l.,
Via Candido Sassone 22/24,
13100 Vercelli, Italy.

Published in 1998 and distributed by
Stewart, Tabori & Chang,
a division of U.S. Media Holdings, Inc.
115 West 18th Street, New York, NY 10011

Distributed in Canada by
General Publishing Company Ltd.
30 Lesmill Road
Don Mills, Ontario, M3B 2T6, Canada

Library of Congress Catalog Card
Number: 97-68224

ISBN 1-55670-690-1

Printed in Italy

10 9 8 7 6 5 4 3 2 1

First Edition

CONTENTS

INTRODUCTION   PAGE   8
BETWEEN HISTORY, LEGEND, AND MYTH   PAGE   20
SPECTACULAR LANDSCAPES SHAPED BY TIME   PAGE   56
THE CITIES OF THE SOUTHWEST:
    A BLEND OF PAST AND FUTURE   PAGE 112
INDEX   PAGE 132

INTRODUCTION

Geronimo and the Grand Canyon; the Rocky Mountains and the Anasazi; the Manhattan Project and Kachina dolls; Navajos and Mormons; the Santa Fe Trail and Cheyenne; the Great Salt Lake; Arches, Canyonlands, Zion, and Capitol Reef national parks; deserts and glaciers; rivers and forests; the Gold Rush; gunfighters; pastures and prairies—all of these make up the American Southwest.

The western frontier's landscape combines natural wonders and geological outrageousness. Wrinkles in the Earth's crust and erosion shaped the broad lands that include the area known as the Four Corners, the point where Arizona, New Mexico, Colorado, and Utah converge. The results are rock arches, canyons, woods, and steep snowy mountains.

History and the men and women who passed through this area have left their mark. In the late 13th century, the Anasazi, the most important prehistoric tribe in the United States, bid farewell to a world that no longer wanted them and, a few centuries before the *Niña*, the *Pinta*, and the *Santa Maria* set out, disappeared into an unknown fate. The Anasazi, or "Old Ones" in the Navajo language, left amazing traces of their existence, including petroglyphs and cliff dwellings, in the walls of the canyons in this region.

The Anasazis' departure opened the Southwest to Native Americans from the north, whom the Europeans called Navajo and Apache. The area also hosted Spanish conquistadors, and missionaries, who were in turn followed by French-speaking trappers, English-speaking mountain men, and Mormons. Gold and silver fever drew miners, adventurers, jailbirds, and dreamers to these lands. The history

8 *Lake Powell is an enormous man-made lake that fills Glen Canyon. The Glen Canyon Dam, promoted by Theodore Roosevelt, is 1,560 feet wide and 710 feet high.*

9 *A rippling dune of red sand stands out against the bold and grandiose cathedrals, while fiery pinnacles reach up to the blue sky. This is Monument Valley, the land of legends and constant challenges.*

of both the West and the Southwest is also dotted with Indian wars, armistices, treaties, reprisals, massacres, and deportations.

The Rocky Mountains are the first obstacle after America's Great Plains. But they were not enough to stop the pioneers, herders, farmers, bankers, and shopkeepers who flooded the area. The incredible rock sculptures at Arches, Black Canyon on the Gunnison River, and the Sonoran Desert looked on as Santa Fe, Tucson, Tombstone, and Cripple Creek grew. The lands where the Jurassic era's dinosaurs once roamed now house the high technology of Salt Lake City and the fighter jets at the Colorado Springs aeronautical academy. But despite the dramatic changes in the region, the Southwest has not lost its charm, its character, or its unique and unforgettable face.

11 top
*The church and
cemetery of the San
Ildefonso pueblo in
New Mexico.*

11 bottom
*Almost all the ghost
towns along the
roads of New Mexico
are abandoned
mining towns.*

*The photograph shows
an old stagecoach
"parked" in front of
the Steins train
station.*

14–15 Every year thousands of visitors travel the winding road that crosses the Navajo tribal lands of Monument Valley. The photograph to the left shows West Mitten, one of the most famous rock formations and the background for innumerable films.

16–17 An organ pipe cactus in Arizona's Sonoran Desert.

18–19 The immensity of the Grand Canyon can be fully appreciated only from the air. Nevertheless, along the South Rim there are twelve scenic observation points that overlook the abyss, offering wonderful panoramas.

Petrified Forest National Park, Arizona

Grand Canyon National Park, Arizona

Bryce Canyon National Park, Utah

California

Il Rio Grande, New Mexico

Old Tucson Studios, Arizona

Pueblo di Taos, New Mexico

Idaho

Nevada

Bringham
City

Great Salt
Lake

Salt Lake City

Great Salt
Lake Desert

Utah
Lake

Utah

Arches National
Park

Colorado

Denver

Bryce Canyon
National Park

Capitol
Reef

Canyonlands
National Park

Colorado

Cedar Breaks

Zion
National Park

Lake
Powell

Glen Canyon
Recreation Area

Mesa Verde
National Park

Rocky Mountains

Sagre De Cristo Mountains

Colorado

Grand Canyon
National Park

Colorado
Plateau

Monument
Valley

Grand Canyon

San Juan

Great Basin
Desert

Rio Chama

Taos

Lake
Mead

Los Alamos

Lake
Havasu

Arizona

Canyon
de Chelly

Santa Fe

Colorado

Phoenix

Petrified Forest
National Park

Albuquerque

Rio Grande

New
Mexico

Gila

Sacramento Mountains

Tucson

Chihuahuan
Desert

White Sand
National Monument

California Gulf

Mexico

13

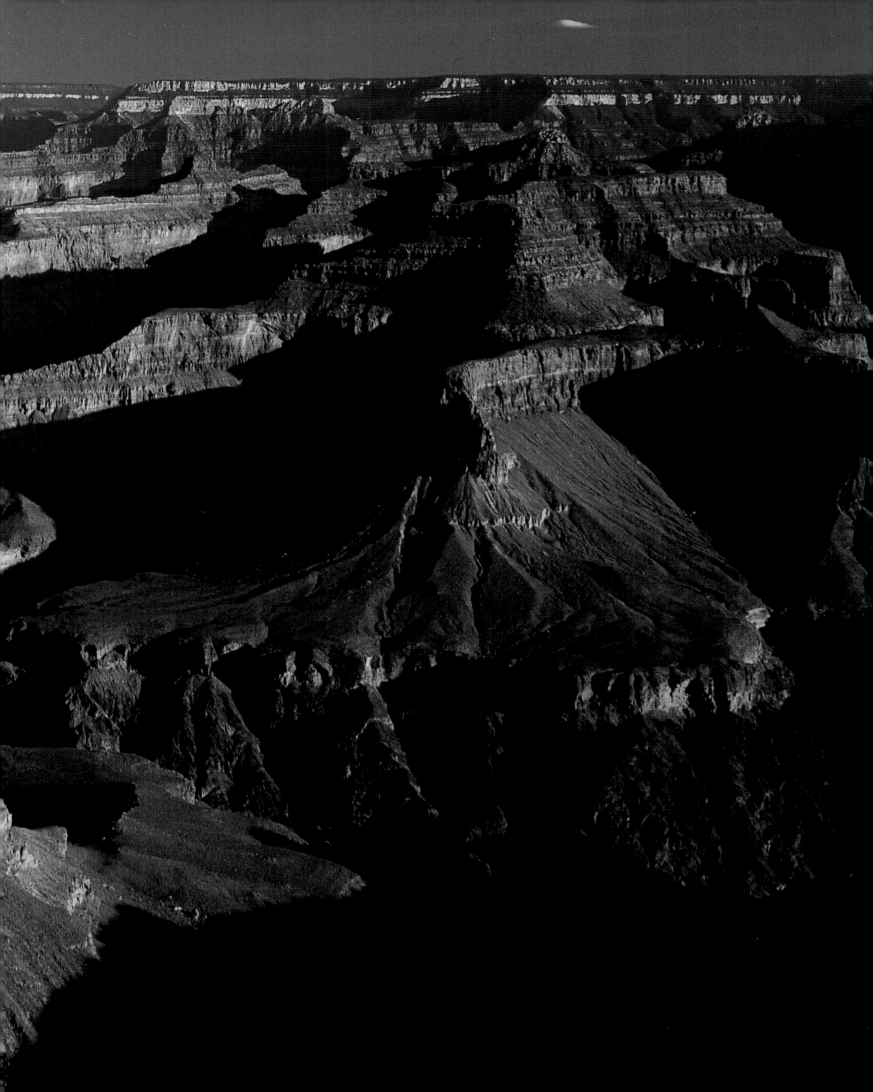

BETWEEN HISTORY, LEGEND, AND MYTH

20–21 *Colorado's Mesa Verde National Park has the remains of human settlements that existed as early as AD 555. This village, which seems almost suspended over the canyon, was inhabited by the Anasazi, a legendary tribe that mysteriously disappeared.*

21 top left *Driven into the mountains, the Anasazi developed a flourishing culture, as can be seen by the numerous artifacts discovered, especially in the Mesa Verde area. In addition to the usual pots and woven articles, there are also shells, copper utensils, and parrot feathers. The photograph shows a woven yucca basket dating back to between 1100 and 1250.*

21 top right *The Anasazis' black-and-white earthenware jars are justly renowned.*

20 *This exquisite little statue, probably dating back to the 13th century, is a vestige of the culture of the Salado Indians, a tribe that, like the Anasazi, lived in cliff dwellings, which offered shelter and protection from enemy attacks.*

*I*f you disturb the sleep of the dead," he warned softly, "you'll die, too." Richard Wetherill felt a chill run up his spine. It was a cold winter morning in December 1888. The land on the Mesa Verde plateau in Colorado was covered with snow, and the air was crisp and pungent. Two men on horseback were climbing up the plateau above Cliff Canyon, their eyes glued to the ground in search of the trail of lost livestock. As they followed the tracks on the ground, Wetherill remembered the words of an old Indian chief. Acowitz was the leader of a small band of Utes. One day, while Wetherill was engrossed in contemplating the curves carved into the rock of Cliff Canyon, which he was seeing for the first time, Acowitz told him something he had never revealed to a white man. At the entry to the gorge were the remains of many buildings built by an ancient people. "The Utes never go there. It is a sacred place, very sacred." While they were returning to their horses, the Indian turned toward Richard. "If you disturb the sleep of the dead," he warned softly, "you'll die, too."

Two years had passed since that exchange, and now, with his brother-in-law Charley Mason, Richard Wetherill was busy with something completely different. Following the tracks of the livestock, the two men reached the border of the plateau and dismounted to climb the steep rocky wall.

An event was about to take place that would bring to light the history of a mysterious people, the Anasazi, the prehistoric Indians of the American Southwest. About a hundred yards ahead, a long rock canopy stretched out to shelter a natural cavern more than 300 feet long and 95 feet wide. Inside the cave were the remains of an ancient city. More than 200 stone and mud buildings, built one on top of another, circled a great round tower three stories high. "It looks like a palace," murmured Charley Mason in amazement.

The two spent the rest of that day reaching the ancient village and digging in the dusty earth that held pottery, woven baskets, and stone and bone tools left by the Anasazis, who had built and lived in those buildings in the 13th century. The dark prophecy of Acowitz never came to pass. Richard Wetherill spent the last 22 years of his life exploring hundreds of canyons in search of other remains. Today, the ruins are among the most impressive prehistoric remains in the United States, and Mesa Verde National Park is visited by a half a million people every year.

Who were the Anasazi? Usually this name is used to identify the people who, during a period roughly between 200 BC and AD 1300, settled the only part of the United States where the boundaries of four states—Utah, Colorado, New Mexico, and Arizona—touch. The word Anasazi is the name the Navajo gave this prehistoric population; it came into common use after it was adopted in 1936 by the archaeologist Alfred V. Kidder.

For centuries, the Anasazi, who are also called "the Old Ones," lived as hunters and gatherers. In the early

22 bottom
The Anasazi life must have been difficult. The cultivated fields, provisions, water, and game were all in the valleys below the pueblos, and Anasazi had to make the difficult descent every morning, with an even harder ascent to bring necessities back up to the dwellings. This photograph shows a jar with a curious zoomorphic form: The jar itself looks like a bird, while a snake crawls up the handle.

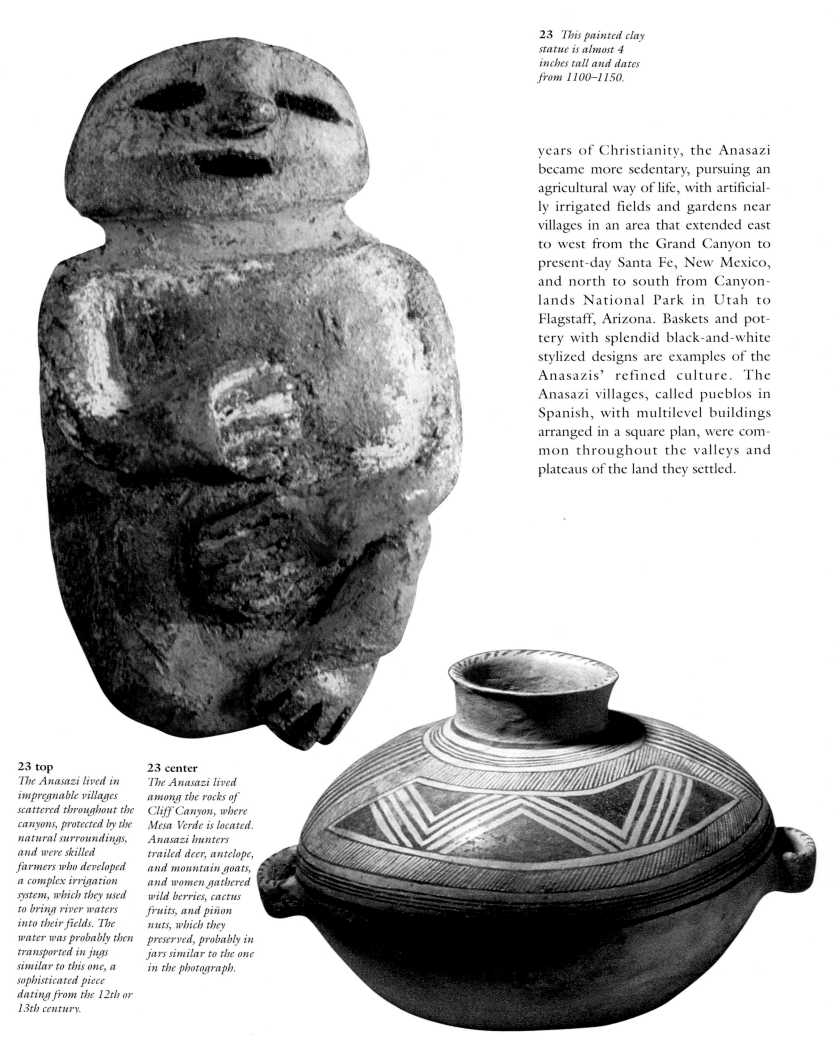

years of Christianity, the Anasazi became more sedentary, pursuing an agricultural way of life, with artificially irrigated fields and gardens near villages in an area that extended east to west from the Grand Canyon to present-day Santa Fe, New Mexico, and north to south from Canyonlands National Park in Utah to Flagstaff, Arizona. Baskets and pottery with splendid black-and-white stylized designs are examples of the Anasazis' refined culture. The Anasazi villages, called pueblos in Spanish, with multilevel buildings arranged in a square plan, were common throughout the valleys and plateaus of the land they settled.

23 top
The Anasazi lived in impregnable villages scattered throughout the canyons, protected by the natural surroundings, and were skilled farmers who developed a complex irrigation system, which they used to bring river waters into their fields. The water was probably then transported in jugs similar to this one, a sophisticated piece dating from the 12th or 13th century.

23 center
The Anasazi lived among the rocks of Cliff Canyon, where Mesa Verde is located. Anasazi hunters trailed deer, antelope, and mountain goats, and women gathered wild berries, cactus fruits, and piñon nuts, which they preserved, probably in jars similar to the one in the photograph.

During the 13th century, there were tens of thousands of Anasazi, and their civilization reached its apex, with villages that had become true cities, sometimes with more than 500 buildings, large boundary walls, and imposing inner squares, all connected by a network of trade and economic and cultural interchange that extended as far as the Pacific and Mexico. Between AD 900 and 1200, Chaco Culture National Historical Park near Bloomfield, New Mexico, was one of the most densely settled regions. At least 5,000 Anasazi lived in large, multilevel stone buildings and cultivated corn and beans in this area.

The Anasazi also built an elaborate road system that connected all 75 pueblos in the region, almost 400 miles of straight roads 30 feet wide, that permitted these communities to trade crops, pottery, and deerskin or buckskin clothing. The great number of *kiva* (underground, circular religious structures) makes it clear that spirituality was central to this ancient civilization. Astronomy was also important to the Anasazi. Observatories scrutinized the elevation and path of the sun, using shafts of light that filtered in from special openings throughout the year. Liturgical ceremonies and agricultural calendars could be planned with accuracy.

Around AD 1000, the Chaco civilization was the religious, political, and economic center of the northwest plateau. Refined agricultural techniques had freed the Anasazi from finding food and allowed them to concentrate on developing their artistic and handicraft abilities. Archaeological excavations have uncovered artifacts from this period: petroglyphs of snakes and spirals, baskets and sandals woven of sturdy desert plants, and domestic and ritual pottery decorated with stylized, black-and-white geometric designs.

Then, right at the apex of the Anasazis' material wealth, something went wrong. The settlements were moved to caves in the canyons, making it not only hard to build houses and religious buildings, but also rendering everyday life harsh. Perhaps the Anasazi made a hasty and desperate search for safety. Perhaps the settlements on the rock walls, the so-called cliff dwellings, were transformed into well-armed defensive bases when the ladders and ropes that facilitated entry were pulled up. What threatened the Anasazi remains a mystery. Many theories have been proposed to explain the disappearance of these people. Current research focuses on climate changes such as the great drought between 1276 and 1299, a calamitous event that has been studied

26 *The red rocks of the Southwest offer testimony to the passage of humankind. This is Canyonlands National Park, and the figures traced by ancient, skilled hands offer abundant information for researchers.*

through an examination of the inner rings of centuries-old trees in the area. Other hypotheses include an accelerated erosion of the soil, caused by massive deforestation, violent epidemics, and a series of ruinous conflicts caused either by outside aggressors or internal destabilizing forces. But perhaps none of these reasons alone provides an adequate reason for the Anasazis' disappearance. Perhaps a number of

factors together may provide the key to the riddle.

Around 1300, all the mountain settlements were abandoned. Those who remained became the present-day Hopi and Pueblo, tribes primarily known for their Kachina dolls. Some Kachinas are guardian spirits that live in lakes, on mountains, and near the sources of rivers, and legend has it that the dolls are responsible for rain, rich harvests, and good health. Other Kachinas belong to a darker world and are demons or evil spirits in charge of punishing errant behavior. In Pueblo myth, the Kachinas were real beings who often visited the people to teach them to hunt, grow crops, and build villages. The Kachinas brought many gifts, and the Pueblos began to take them for granted, thus losing respect and veneration for them. After a number of serious conflicts, the Kachina

27 The Island in the Sky area, in the southern portion of Canyonlands National Park, is famous for its views and its petroglyphs. This photograph shows Newspaper Rock, so named because of the wealth of "news" it contains.

stopped visiting the people, but before they left, they taught a group of Pueblos, who had remained faithful, sacred ceremonies and dances and the art of making masks and costumes.

The Hohokam tribe faced a fate similar to that of the Anasazi. From AD 450, the tribes of the Hohokam culture cultivated the valleys in the area between present-day Phoenix and Casa Grande. Over the next millennium the Hohokam built a network of canals that extended for more than 600 miles, a portion of

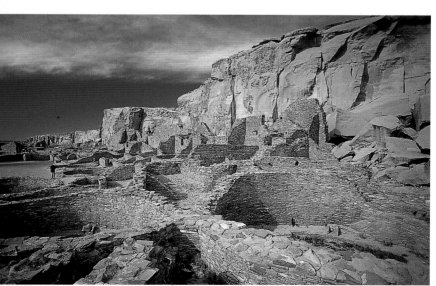

which is still visible today. Although Hohokam culture was quite advanced, it left little trace of its passage because Hohokam buildings were built of clay, which erodes quickly. The tribe created many petroglyphs, and recent studies have shown that rock carvings marked important astronomical events such as the solstices and equinoxes, fundamental dates in the sacred, esoteric calendar of ancient civilizations. The Hohokam dammed the Salt River as early as the 4th century AD. Around AD 1100, Hohokam settlements reached a population of between 50,000 and 100,000 people, and the culture was one of the most sophisticated and advanced cultures north of Mexico. The Hohokam were responsible for the introduction of cotton and weaving throughout the Southwest. For more than 1,500 years, the Hohokam occupied the area, until they, too, mysteriously disappeared around 1450. The Pima Indians later settled on the lands of those they called *Hohokam*, "those who left."

28 top
Chaco Canyon is one of the most important archaeological sites in North America. The area contains traces of the sophisticated Anasazi civilization, with its advanced architecture.

28 center and bottom and 29
The heart of Chaco Culture National Park is Pueblo Bonito, the most important Anasazi city. It reveals the civilization's advanced culture and urban development. Of special note are the complex irrigation systems, the dwellings, and the wide streets.

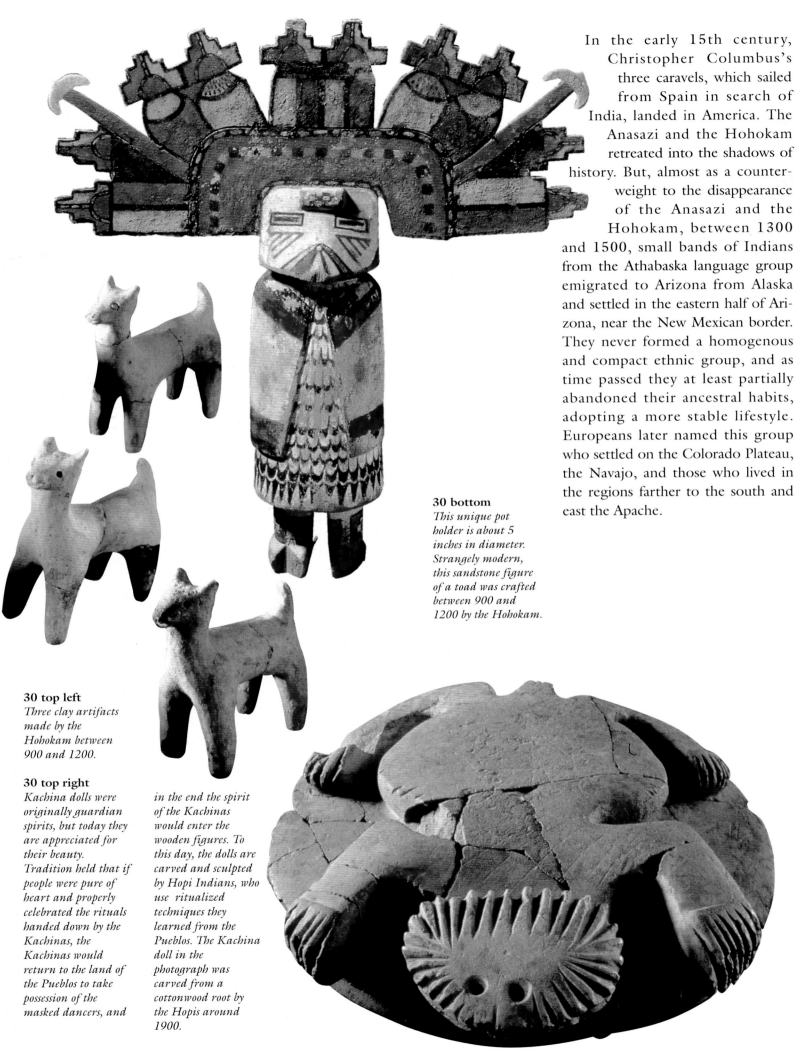

In the early 15th century, Christopher Columbus's three caravels, which sailed from Spain in search of India, landed in America. The Anasazi and the Hohokam retreated into the shadows of history. But, almost as a counter-weight to the disappearance of the Anasazi and the Hohokam, between 1300 and 1500, small bands of Indians from the Athabaska language group emigrated to Arizona from Alaska and settled in the eastern half of Arizona, near the New Mexican border. They never formed a homogenous and compact ethnic group, and as time passed they at least partially abandoned their ancestral habits, adopting a more stable lifestyle. Europeans later named this group who settled on the Colorado Plateau, the Navajo, and those who lived in the regions farther to the south and east the Apache.

30 bottom
This unique pot holder is about 5 inches in diameter. Strangely modern, this sandstone figure of a toad was crafted between 900 and 1200 by the Hohokam.

30 top left
Three clay artifacts made by the Hohokam between 900 and 1200.

30 top right
Kachina dolls were originally guardian spirits, but today they are appreciated for their beauty. Tradition held that if people were pure of heart and properly celebrated the rituals handed down by the Kachinas, the Kachinas would return to the land of the Pueblos to take possession of the masked dancers, and in the end the spirit of the Kachinas would enter the wooden figures. To this day, the dolls are carved and sculpted by Hopi Indians, who use ritualized techniques they learned from the Pueblos. The Kachina doll in the photograph was carved from a cottonwood root by the Hopis around 1900.

31 top
The skilled craftsmanship of the early Anasazi was probably passed to all Indian cultures. The photograph shows two jars from different areas, both crafted in the early 20th century. The amphora to the left, 8 inches in diameter and about 6 inches high, was found at San Ildefonso Pueblo, New Mexico, and the jar to the right comes from Cochiti Pueblo, New Mexico.

31 center left
These two Hohokam artifacts from Snaketown, Arizona, date from 900–1150 and may have served as ritual cups. They depict a man (left) and a woman (right).

31 center right
The figurative art of the Indian civilizations in the American Southwest is priceless. This colorful jar from Acoma Pueblo dates to the late 19th century.

Spanish colonization is a critical piece of the Southwest's past. Spanish culture dominated the area for about three centuries, from the mid-16th century to the mid-19th century. The effects of Spanish culture and civilization are stronger in present-day New Mexico because Mexico was the oldest and most populous province of the viceroyalty of New Spain.

31 bottom
This figure of a woman dates from the late Anasazi era, at the beginning of Hopi domination, between 1400 and 1600.

After initial conflicts, Spanish settlers coexisted with the indigenous tribes. The Spanish had no racial prejudices, and the cultural exchange between the groups was extensive and fruitful and included medicine, agricultural methods, architecture, domestic animals, and ways of cooking meat, fish, bread, beans, and chili. Almost every conquistador watered his horses on the banks of the "great river," the Rio Grande, as it was called by the awed Spaniards.

On February 22, 1540, 336 horsemen, 600 horses, a group of missionaries, and about 100 Indians with flocks of sheep, goats, and other livestock set out from Compostela, the capital of Nueva Galicia, 500 miles north of Mexico City, in an expedition led by Francisco Vásquez de Coronado beyond the northern borders of the Spanish colonial empire. Coronado returned in 1542. He had not found cities of gold, jewels, or wealth. But he had discovered the Grand Canyon, reached the Hawikuh pueblo of the Zuni Indians near Gallup, and continued east toward Tiguex near Santa Fe, where he set up winter camp. In the spring, he ventured out to the Great Plains, looking for hidden treasures in Quivira, in present-day Kansas, where he found only the grass huts of the Wichita tribes. To his contemporaries, Coronado's expedition was a failure, but the Spanish explorer was responsible for bringing horses to the Great Plains of North America, teaching Indians European agricultural techniques, introducing animal husbandry to the area's peoples, and making cartographers aware of enormous, hitherto unknown regions.

32 Francisco Vásquez de Coronado, the governor of the northern provinces of New Spain, went to Mexico in 1535 in hopes of finding new riches. In February 1540, Coronado, leading about 300 soldiers as well as missionaries and Indians and their pack animals and livestock, left in search of the legendary Seven Cities of Cibola, the famous cities of gold recounted by the Franciscan monk Marco da Nizza. The missionary had reported marvelous tales to Mendoza, the viceroy of Mexico: stone buildings 10 stories high and temples covered with turquoise. What Coronado found was quite another thing: pueblos sheltered in the hills and the huts of the Indians of the Great Plains.

32–33 This 16th-century painting by the Dutch artist Jan Mostaert shows Spanish troops attacking a Zuni pueblo. The painting was based on the painter's imagination and not an eyewitness account of the tragic events. The country, in particular the trees and animals, are clearly European, as are the naked and bearded Indians. The village, which resembles those sheltered on the mesas, is more realistic.

The first serious Spanish attempt to colonize New Mexico was organized in 1598 by Juan de Oñate, who brought with him 130 soldiers, 400 settlers, 7,000 head of livestock, and a group of priests—the first trickle of European immigration that was destined to change the fate of the continent. Six months after leaving Mexico, Oñate and his men stopped in a valley where the Rio Grande and the Chama River met and began to build San Gabriel, the first state capital.

Este cuadro, que el Instituto de Cultura Hispánica ofrece al Museo de Nuevo México, es copia del verdadero retrato de D. Diego Vargas Zapata, de la Casa de los Vargas, cuyo original se conserva en la capilla de San Isidro sita en el Pueblo de Santisteban de Madrid.

Life in the Southwest remained largely unchanged until 1610, when Pedro de Peralta arrived. This time, the arriving settlers intended to transfer their culture, religion, traditions of government, lifestyles, and organization of labor to the new lands. Peralta built the new capital at Santa Fe, which he called *Villa Real de la Santa Fe de San Francisco de Asis*, the Royal City of the Holy Faith of Saint Francis of Assisi.

In the 17th century, the southernmost part of the Southwest came under the influence of missionaries, who felt it was their duty to transform the Indian tribes into Christian farmers. The work of Spanish missionaries in southern Arizona was organized primarily by Eusebio Francisco Kino, an Italian Jesuit educated in Germany, who settled among the Pima tribes. He taught them European agricultural practices and gave the indigenous peoples livestock to raise.

But abuses committed by Spanish settlers rendered the efforts of the Jesuits unsuccessful and led to a revolt by the Pima in 1751. The Europeans reacted by setting up a permanent mission in Tumacacori and military fortifications at Tubac. In 1756, San Francisco was founded, and the Tubac fortress was transferred to Tucson, where Father Kino laid the foundations of the San Xavier del Bac mission. Although they had rebelled in 1680, the Pueblo quickly converted to Christianity. In 1692, Diego de Vargas reconquered Santa Fe but did not punish rebellious tribes, thus accelerating conversions. By the end of the century, the entire territory was under Spanish control. The authorities and the settlers became more tolerant of indigenous peoples and guaranteed them great autonomy in self-governance.

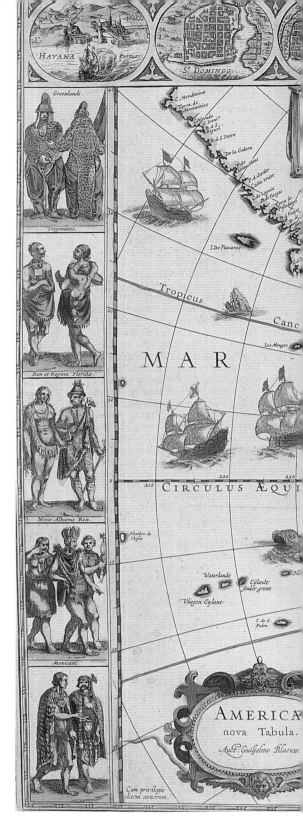

34 top
Juan de Oñate, who
lived from 1549 to
1624, was New
Mexico's first settler.
He left Mexico to lead
a group of settlers
(130 families),
missionaries, and
soldiers, and headed

toward the Rio
Grande Valley
to go up the river.
He found an ideal
site for the city of San
Gabriel, which he
founded at the
confluence of the Rio
Grande and Chama
rivers.

34 bottom
Spanish general
Diego de Vargas
spearheaded Europe's
reconquest of New
Mexico after the
Pueblo revolt. He
suppressed the
rebellion without
using force—it is said

that he never used an
ounce of gunpowder
or bloodied his
sword—and
facilitated the
rapid conversion
to Christianity of
the Indian tribes
he subjected.

34–35 This map of
the American
continent, done by
W.J. Biaeu around
1650, shows the
southern part of North
America that was
occupied by the
Spanish.

In 1821, Mexico gained independence from Spain, and Tucson, with 65 inhabitants, became part of the new country, which at that time extended to northern California, including parts of Colorado, Wyoming, and New Mexico. In 1848, after the war with the United States, the Treaty of Guadalupe Hidalgo ceded to the United States the territory between California and Texas, which became the New Mexico Territory.

36 top right
After gaining its independence from the Spanish, between 1846 and 1848 Mexico ceded a large part of its northern territories to the United States. The picture shows a moment from the battle of Mill Elrey, near Mexico City.

36 bottom right
The American flag unfurls above a scene of suffering and death during the Battle of Chapultepec on September 18, 1847. This was one of the many battles fought to gain independence from Mexico.

37 *With their swords drawn and lances raised, a group of Mexican soldiers is near defeat during the Battle of Buena Vista, which was fought on February 23, 1847.*

38 left
After the Civil War, adventurers in search of fortune swarmed over the gold mines and fields of central Arizona. The pioneers, often accompanied by their families, encountered many difficulties along the way, but they succeeded in overcoming every obstacle.

The gold rush of 1849 and the forty-niners it brought with it played their part in settling Arizona, where a rich deposit of gold was discovered in 1857. After gold, silver, copper, and lead were found in Utah and Colorado, large groups of immigrants settled in the Southwest, followed by farmers and livestock breeders eager to collect the proceeds of the rich and seemingly boundless mining market.

Mining cities arose out of nowhere, flourishing until the vein was exhausted, when the cities were just as quickly abandoned to become ghost towns. Frontier cities sprang up full of the vices and violence associated with sudden and uncontrolled wealth: gambling halls, brothels, saloons, and gunfights in the street. The dubious epic of the West can be summed up in two names destined to become famous as the wildest cities of the United States: Bisbee and Tombstone, where the gunfight at the OK Corral, the most famous in the West, took place. During this period, the Southwest was a land of cowboys, miners, sheriffs, outlaws, lynchings, and train robberies—a legacy of violence immortalized by thousands of modern-day Western films. The tumultuous age of the frontier had begun.

38 right
The history of the West began with the first wagonloads of settlers who headed out from the East Coast and Europe to challenge the natural barriers of the canyons and thread their way across the endless prairie to the new promised land. The picture on top shows a caravan traveling along the Columbia River.

39 The dream of gold and quick fortunes inspired a multitude of adventurers to venture into the wild and hostile lands of the Southwest. The miners established the foundations for new communities. The pictures show a hill literally disemboweled to extract the precious metal (top); a typical old gold miner with his thick beard, mules, and sieve (center); and (below) a mine built during the late 19th century using the most modern techniques of the period.

40 top

The first cowboys to reach the harsh, desolate lands of the West had few distractions. The day was almost always dedicated to the hard work of conquering the land. This picture shows a typical scene of the period: A cowboy with a large Colt in his pocket attempts to subdue a rebellious horse.

40 center

There were not many diversions for the first pioneers in the West. The only place to go for relaxation was the saloon, a meeting place where people could exchange information, make new friends, and socialize.

40 bottom

During the conquest of the West, many banks coined their own money to encourage commercial trade. This dollar for herdsmen was minted by a bank in Salt Lake City, Utah.

41 *Cowboy life has become famous through the many unforgettable films featuring no-nonsense actors like John Wayne, who starred in numerous cowboy adventures. The cowboys, many of whom responded to the 1859 cry of the New York Tribune to "Go West, Young Man," succeeded in conquering the land, thus laying the foundations for the great American nation. The photographs show a group of cowboys at mealtime (top), a herd being led through the wild canyons of Arizona (center), and an old cowboy on his faithful mount with a big lasso.*

42 top and left

After the arrival of troops in the early 1800s, settlers, businessmen, cowboys, gunslingers, sheriffs, and outlaws began to settle in the Southwest, all in the best tradition of the American frontier. There are endless stories of robberies, murders, and outrages from this period in American history. The photographs show some of the protagonists of one of the most memorable shootouts: the OK Corral. The shoot-out, which occurred in 1881 in the city of Tombstone (top left), was a confrontation between corrupt authorities accused of cattle rustling, represented by the sheriff Wyatt Earp (below left), and the more peaceful ranchers, the Clanton and Frank brothers (top left), and Thomas McLaury (top right).

42 top right
William Bonney, better known as Billy the Kid, was a legendary figure of the West in the 1880s.

42 bottom right
Women used weapons to protect themselves from the hardships of the West. This is Calamity Jane.

43 top left
With his creased hat, neckerchief, boots, spurs, and rifle in hand, Sheriff William Pinkerton (center) poses with two deputies.

43 bottom left
Although they dressed especially for this photograph, these famous bandits kept their pistols in their belts and their rifles in hand. This is the Jesse James gang: From left to right are Cole Younger, Jesse James, Bob Younger, and Frank James.

43 right
Stagecoach attacks and train robberies were two dangers that sometimes threatened the lives, and always endangered the wallets, of the new conquerors of the West.

The United States adopted a position toward native peoples that was much less tolerant than that of the Spanish and Mexicans. Authorities in Washington felt they had a manifest destiny to colonize North America from one ocean to the other. And native peoples and culture paid dearly for it.

44 left
An 1891 lithograph of a fight among four trappers and a group of Indians.

44 top right
This 19th-century lithograph shows Red River Hunters Indian camp.

44 bottom right
Native Americans, armed with only bows and arrows, attack a stagecoach. The stagecoach was a fundamental means of transportation for delivering mail from the East.

45 top left

The extermination of the Indians was brutal and unforgivable. Public notices were posted to recruit men to pillage everything the indigenous tribes had, from their land to their horses.

45 top right

In this painting by Newell Convers Wyeth, a group of Indians armed with lances and arrows, their faces smeared with the traditional war paint, is preparing to launch an assault on the cavalry.

45 center

This picture from Le Petit Journal of February 25, 1906, shows a group of rifle-toting Indians attacking a train in Arizona.

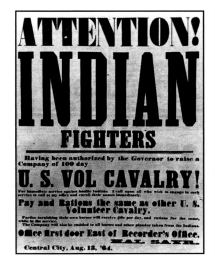

45 bottom

A group of soldiers and trappers, easily recognizable by their fringed leather jackets, hides along the banks of a river as they await the attack of a multitude of Indians.

The struggle between the Apache and the U.S. government was only one of the many conflicts in the history of the Southwest and the western frontier, a chronicle of painful tragedies that repeated itself over and over again.

In 1898, Geronimo, the last great Apache warrior, wrote, "I have been far from my land for twelve years. The trees and the rivers, the mountains and the desert are asking where I have gone. They need me. They want me to return home." He wanted to return home to die and be buried in the mountains of Arizona, the land of his fathers, for which he had fought fiercely. His request was denied. On a winter night in 1909, as he returned home from the city in Lawton, Oklahoma, Geronimo fell from his horse into a ditch. Four days later, nearly 86 years old, he died of pneumonia.

Goyahkla, Geronimo's given name, was born into the Apache tribe of the Chiricahua about 1829. The event that would change his life

occurred in 1882 in Janos, a city in the Mexican state of Chihuahua, when a platoon of Mexican troops from the nearby state of Sonora came upon the Indian camp. They killed 25 women and children, and another 60 Apache people were captured and sold as slaves. When Geronimo returned home toward evening, he found his mother, wife, and three children among the bodies. As he was mourning his dead, Geronimo received shamanic powers: He heard a voice telling him that from that moment on, bullets could no longer kill him. He then began his private war against the Mexicans. The first

47 top
When Geronimo's band of Long Knives finally surrendered (Geronimo is in the first row, third from the right), it included

16 warriors, 12 women, and 6 children. They had battled 5,000 U.S. soldiers, a quarter of the entire army, and about 3,000 Mexican

soldiers. The great Apache chief's resistance came to an end, and with it the freedom of the Indians.

47 bottom
Geronimo shows the effects of many years of battles and defeats.

Spanish-speaking victims of the Apache warrior gave him the nickname that would go down in history, when they watched him raging unharmed through clouds of bullets. Terrorized as they saw him racing toward them untouched by the whizzing bullets, they began to invoke the name of Saint Jerome, *Geronimo* in Spanish. After 10 years of battling with the Apaches of Cochise, the federal government decided that the solution to the Indian problem was to set up Indian reservations. The government and its representatives signed a series of solemn promises, all of which were broken by the federal authorities. The Apache and Native holocaust had begun.

48 top
The courageous pioneers traveled about 1,860 miles in a single summer to reach the promised land of the West. This photograph, taken in 1882, shows a group of wagons slowly moving through the inhospitable, sunbaked lands.

48 center
The pioneers endured a hard life. The members of two families pose for a picture during a stop on their long trek across the Great Plains.

48 bottom
Conestoga wagons not only transported goods, but also functioned as true mobile homes.

The conquest of the new lands continued, and the pioneers' covered wagons headed west along the Santa Fe and Mormon trails. The Santa Fe Trail began at Franklin, Missouri, but after repeated flooding of the river, it was moved to Lexington, and then to Independence; it ended at Santa Fe, New Mexico, 868 miles away. But the influence of the Santa Fe Trail extended well beyond the road itself. The trading market extended from Missouri all the way to Europe, a source of textiles prepared expressly for sale outside Mexico. The era of the Santa Fe Trail ended when the first train entered the Santa Fe station on February 9, 1880. The iron rails would erase the tracks of mules and oxen and Conestoga wagons.

During the 19th century, the Southwest saw the creation of Utah by the Mormon church, nourished by floods of immigrants along the Mormon Trail. The cracking whips, creaking wheels, clattering hooves of the animals pulling the wagons, and hymns of the Church of the Latter-

Day Saints accompanied one of the most amazing mass migrations in the history of the United States. The Mormon church was not looked upon favorably in the United States. In July 1844, after Joseph Smith died in Carthage at the hands of an angry mob in the building where he had been jailed with his brother, Hiram, and other leaders, Brigham Young, the new Mormon leader, decided that it was time to move his followers to more hospitable lands in the Rocky Mountain territory in the valley of the Great Salt Lake. Nothing could slow the implacable march of the 70,000 Mormons who

49 *The trail the pioneers blazed to the West started from Missouri and crossed mountains and deserts, with all types of hardship, before reaching Santa Fe.*

The Santa Fe Trail witnessed the hopes, bitter defeats, and stirring joys of entire generations of people, like these shown in the photographs.

50 top
The dream of new lands drove the Mormons west. They were not attracted by the wealth of the North American West, with its gold, furs, and acres of cheap land, nor by the thirst for adventure or glory. If it had been up to them, they *would never have gone west at all. But once the decision was made, they set out to accomplish their task with stubborn determination. This 1862 engraving shows Joseph Smith, the Mormon prophet, preaching to a group of Indians.*

traveled the 1,297 miles that separated Nauvoo, Illinois, from the Salt Lake Valley. The Mormon Trail ended at Salt Lake City and remained a vital roadway for Mormon immigration for more than 20 years.

Then, a brief message changed the destiny of the West: "The last rail is down and the last nail is in place. The Pacific Railroad is finished." The telegram sent to President Grant on May 10, 1869, announced the joining of the iron rails in Promontory, Utah, connecting the east and west coasts of the United States. On July 1, 1862, President Abraham Lincoln signed the Pacific Railroad Act, which authorized the Central Pacific to lay its rails east of Sacramento and the Union Pacific to begin work west

51 bottom left
The cupola of the temple dominating a bustling Salt Lake City in 1867.

51 bottom right
Brigham Young, the Mormon leader who chose Salt Lake for his new community.

50–51 *This curious map shows the Mormons' route. Because of growing tensions with the local population, the Mormons left Nauvoo for the Great Salt Lake early in the year, exposing the immigrants to the rigors of a still-frigid winter and making the advance of the wagons even more difficult. The first* *group of Mormon pioneers included 143 men, 3 women, and 2 children. Divided into groups of 50 and 10, they had 72 wagons, 93 horses, 66 oxen, 52 mules, 19 cows, 17 dogs, and a few chickens. About 1,055 miles stood between this handful of adventurers and the Salt Lake Valley.*

52 top
With modern technologies and the arrival of the railroads and the telegraph, the western territories drew closer to those of the East. The construction of the railroad used thousands of

immigrants, especially Chinese, and had to overcome enormous obstacles and unexpected difficulties. This picture shows a group of men working on the construction of a bridge over a tumultuous river.

52-53 *On May 10, 1869, the two branches of the railroad met at Promontory, Utah. This photograph shows engineers, laborers, and technicians toasting the beginning of a new era.*

53 top
A group of coolies, recognizable by their unmistakable clothing and straw hats, poses on a railroad trolley. This is one of the rare pictures of the builders of the Transcontinental Railroad.

of Omaha, Nebraska. The Central Pacific began construction on January 8, 1863, in Sacramento. The Union Pacific used Irish labor, but Charles Crocker, one of the owners of the Central Pacific, contracted Chinese immigrants, who were beginning to arrive in the building yards by the thousands. The railroad was built by 10,000 coolies, who were scorched by the sun and stung by the cold and who labored day after day, month after month, year after year. But in the photograph of the historic joining of the two railroad lines in Promontory, Utah, on May 10, 1869, not a single Chinese is visible among the celebrating crowds. The railroad, the symbol of progress and modernity for the development of the United States, triggered a chain reaction that cast a disquieting shadow.

On January 6, 1912, New Mexico became the 47th state in the Union. The years passed, and in the midst of World War II, secret laboratories were set up in Los Alamos. Scientists from all over the United States gathered in the mountain city near Santa Fe to conduct research on the top-secret Manhattan Project. Los Alamos was the uneasy cradle of the contemporary world. The atom bomb was created here, on Pajarito Plateau, between the Jemez Mountains and the Rio Grande Valley, 33 miles northwest of Santa Fe. The director of the Manhattan Project, J. Robert Oppenheimer, and about a hundred scientists began work in April

53 center
The spartan lodgings of the men who built the railroad. Often, soldiers with large cannon accompanied the laborers to protect them and the railroad from Indian attacks.

53 bottom
This elaborate poster heralds the opening of the railroad.

54 *The city of Los Alamos, New Mexico, holds an important, if uncomfortable, place in the history of the Southwest and the world. This is where the secret Manhattan Project was carried out, ending with the development of the atom bomb. These pictures show the director of the project, J. Robert Oppenheimer, on the site of the explosion of July 16, 1945 (top), and the terrible, apocalyptic mushroom cloud that rose up in the desert at Trinity Site.*

1943. The apocalypse was designed where the Anasazi once lived and where mountain lions, elk, and bears once roamed. On July 16, 1945, at Trinity Site, in the desert waste of Journada del Muerto, Oppenheimer and his team exploded the world's first nuclear bomb. The team referred to the bomb as the "Fat Man." From that moment, on the world has had to live with the nightmare of nuclear apocalypse.

55 left
Shiny metal structures and men in white shirts have taken over Los Alamos, which was once inhabited by the Anasazi.

55 right
The director of the Manhattan Project, J. Robert Oppenheimer. The scientist led a group of about 100 experts who, starting in 1943, worked for about two years on creating and refining the atom bomb.

56 top
*These aerial views
show the red lands of
the Grand Canyon
and the green water
of the Colorado
River, which over the
course of thousands of
years has carved this
deep fissure into the
earth.*

56–57 and 57
The Colorado River is not the only force responsible for the Grand Canyon. The plateau across which the river flows continues to grow even today, and while the Colorado continues to carve its way down through the bed of rock, the walls of the gorge continue to increase in height.
The image of a knife slicing through a cake is usually used to illustrate the tectonic phenomenon that created the Grand Canyon. But the movement needs to be inverted, because the cake is moving up against the knife rather than the knife cutting down through the cake.

*B*right Angel, Temple of Vishnu, Hindu Amphitheater, Wotan's Throne, Siegfried's Pyre, Temple of Apollo, Tower of Ra, Osiris Peak: The toponymy of Grand Canyon National Park's geologic syncretism seems to include every known religion. A masterpiece of natural sculpture and one of the most revealing chapters in the autobiography of our planet, the Grand Canyon of the Colorado River, 276 miles long, 18 miles wide, and 5,200 feet deep, is a definitive break in the physical and geological continuity of two regions of northern Arizona, known as the North Rim and the South Rim. The national park that preserves their integrity extends from Lake Mead, between Arizona and Nevada, almost to Lake Powell on the Utah border. But these facts will not prepare any visitor for the first sight of this immense spectacle.

The canyon is an extraordinary sculpture modeled by erosion. A descent into the Colorado gorge means venturing into the vortex of geological history. Visiting the Grand Canyon is a true undertaking: From Williams, you climb toward the 6,890-foot-high South Rim across the Coconino Plateau and the Kaibab National Forest, full of junipers, Gambel oaks, tall, sturdy ponderosa pines with their orange color and vanilla-scented bark, and piñon pines, smaller and less graceful than ponderosas but always extremely useful for the Native American populations. The Grand Canyon also has impressive layers of rock, which are made of particles that were transported by wind and water and settled and accumulated to form a layer of sedimentation.

The layers in the canyon are a geologic clock. Just as the rings within a tree trunk tell their story, the layers of rock brought to the surface by the erosion produced by the Colorado River offer a clear chronology that goes back to the most ancient eras known to geologists. Experts

Shortly after the end of World War I, Ferdinand Foch, the former supreme commander of the Allied forces, visited the Grand Canyon. A swarm of reporters followed the French leader, eager to report the Foch's impressions.

It is said that Foch gazed for some time at the immense gorge yawning open before him, then murmured: "The canyon is the greatest manifestation of the presence of God on the face of the earth."

59 top
During the winter months, an often-thick layer of snow lies on the red rocks of the Grand Canyon.

believe it took about 10 million years to create the Grand Canyon. In Granite Gorge, the Colorado flows between sheer cliffs that rise as much as 4,920 feet, deeply embanked in a type of very hard, almost black rock known as Vishnu schist, one of the most ancient rocks ever found on Earth, originating 2 billion years ago.

In the Grand Canyon, antiquity is paired with great biological diversity. The canyon is characterized by a remarkable variety of climates that can encourage or significantly block the development of various forms of animal and plant life. The temperature on the northern plateau is on the average 65°F lower than that at the bottom of the spectacular gorge. In February, snow on the North Rim can be several feet deep, while the snow that falls into the dry heat of the abyss melts immediately. Because of the mild temperatures, the banks of the Colorado are often covered with flowers.

For more than 6 million years, the Colorado River has worked ceaselessly to open a path all along its course, digging, shaping, and carrying away the crumbled remains of its impressive work. With its tributaries, the Dirty Devil, the Escalante, the San Juan, and the Green rivers, the drainage system of the Colorado River has created a broad network sculpted out of the territory that extends to the most remote

60–61 *The oldest rocks found in the Grand Canyon are more than 2 billion years old.*

**62–63 and
63 top left**
*There are 2,000
natural arches in
Arches National
Park, located in
southern Utah, just a
little north of the
winding Colorado
River.*

63 top right
*Although the park
looks like a desert
and the red sandstone
pinnacles capture
everyone's attention,
wildlife survives in
this inhospitable area.*

62 *The Colorado
Plateau, the great
high plain carved by
the Colorado River,
is characterized by
an incredible natural
architecture.
These photographs
show several of the
numerous natural
arches that can be
found in Arches
National Park.*

corners of the plateau that bears its name. The Colorado River, a giant that unfurls its ribbon of shining waters for 1,444 miles, from the Rocky Mountains northwest of Denver to the Gulf of California in Mexico, crosses the Colorado Plateau, 109 million acres of land that radiate out from the Four Corners area of the United States. The plateau rises from 2,000 to 12,000 feet above sea level, is composed primarily of sedimentary rock, and covers southeast Utah, southwest Colorado, northwest New Mexico, and northeast Arizona. The Colorado Plateau's incredible scenery is dominated by the outlandish and extravagant forms of the red rock. The evolution of the landscape was caused by the rising of the Earth's crust and by erosion. Thus were formed the rock sculptures in these world-famous national parks and monuments: Zion, Canyonlands and Capitol Reef, as well as Glen Canyon, Rainbow Bridge, Dead Horse Point, and Arches National Park. The chisel that carved these works of rocky macramé was water, which percolates through the layers of sandstone.

64–65 *Geology professors note that rock is not a solid substance. Rocks in Arches National Park give the impression of being solid, but the forces that control their disintegration, or transformation, are always at work. The lichen that frequently appears on the rocky walls is a fundamental agent of erosion, because it retains humidity and creates a chemical reaction that transforms it into an organic acid that erodes the limestone.*

66 *Threatening clouds overhang the red earth of Arches National Park, but no rain will touch this arid land.*

67–70 *Soft red sandstone deposited more than 150 million years ago on a vast desert provided the raw materials for the arches and pinnacles of Arches National Park.*

71 *Arches National Park is visited by about 500,000 people every year. The best time to visit the park is in the spring or winter, when* *temperatures are not excessively warm or cold, the park is not as crowded, and unforgettable hikes are possible.*

72–73 and 73 top
*Canyonlands
National Park was
established in Utah in
1964 and is another
testimony to the
incredible evolution
that the Earth has*

*undergone over time.
The rocks, are
striated with light
and dark colors, a
reminder of the
millions of years that
have passed.*

Canyonlands National Park is the most tortuous and spectacular section of the Colorado Plateau. Seen from above, the park looks like a series of fractures, abysses, ravines, gorges, tunnels, and towers swathed in the softest tones of ocher sandstone. There are thousands of canyons in the Southwest. One of the most beautiful was carved out by Oak Creek. The background for numerous westerns, Oak Creek Canyon is located near Sedona in central Arizona, 93 miles north of Phoenix. It is said that no other region of the United States has such beautiful natural scenery in such a small space.

Delimited by Magollon Rim, central Arizona includes the beautiful, fertile valley of the Verde River, Oak Creek Canyon, the vermilion rocks of Sedona, pine forests around Prescott, and desert near Wickenburg. This portion of the Grand Canyon State played an important role in history and has a great variety of landscapes and different natural environments. Bell Rock, Cathedral Rock, Courthouse, Eagle Head, Twin Nuns, and Mother and Child are some of the area's most famous rock formations.

72 top
*Prickly shrubs
conquer the dry
red earth in
Canyonlands
National Park.
Although this area
receives only about
4 inches of
precipitation a year,
many species of plants
grow here.*

72 bottom
*A puma waiting to
attack an incautious
prey.*

75 right
Geological forces at work for at least 330 million years forged the hard rocks of Natural Bridge Park. In this

protected area are walls sculpted and furrowed by time and three natural arches at three different stages of development and erosion.

74 and 75 bottom left
In Arizona, also known as the Grand Canyon State, the landscape is ever-changing. The photographs show the imposing formations of Cathedral Rock.

75 top left
The mountains behind Sedona, Arizona. Much of Sedona's attraction lies in the particular geology of the region. The rocks here have seven different sedimentary layers.

Arizona's Canyon de Chelly is one of the most beautiful sheltered rock fortresses in the world, carved into the plateau by the combined forces of wind and water. The canyon's name comes from the Spanish mispronunciation of a Navajo word, *tsegi*, which means "rocky canyon." The canyon's rocks were sculpted into forms that are almost as spectacular and monumental as the Grand Canyon. Its beauty is stark and pure, almost absolute, perhaps disquieting, and certainly extreme. Here nature speaks with the power and voice of the deserts, of impregnable mountains, of stormy seas, of tropical hurricanes. It leaves no room for pastels.

Other fantastic landscapes sculpted by erosion are located in southern Utah, in a sliver of the United States framed clearly by Aquarius Plateau to the west, the Le Sal Mountains to the east, San Rafael Swell to the northwest, and Book Cliffs to the northeast. Along Utah's southeast border lie Comb Ridge and the San Juan River, and to the southwest, Zion and Bryce Canyon national parks, Capitol Reef, and Kaiparowits Plateau.

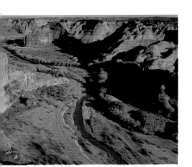

77 *The Anasazi left traces of their passage in Canyon de Chelly. The canyon has archaeological evidence of about 400 settlements, including primitive pit houses, circular underground houses with an entry on the roof, and brick structures up to three stories high, dating from a period around AD 1280. The Anasazi left thousands of paintings on the canyon walls, in a hermetic and symbolic language of ritual, art and culture. Following their example, the Navajo began to settle Canyon de Chelly around the mid-18th century.*

78–79 *Paria Canyon is protected by Paria Canyon Vermilion Cliff Wilderness Area, a natural park established in 1984. This Arizona park covers a surface area of about 108,680 acres and was sculpted and shaped by the Paria River over the millennia.*

80–81 and 81
Incredible pinnacles that seem to challenge all physical laws, immense amphitheaters stretching out, and brilliantly colored rocks blend into a unique landscape in Bryce Canyon National Park. The park, which is located in Utah and opened in 1928, is an amphitheater dug into Paunsaugunt Plateau, or "Beaver House" in the language of local Indian tribes.

82–83 *A delicate layer of snow lies on the red pinnacles of Bryce Amphitheater, creating an incredible contrast of light and color.*

84 top and 84–85
Glen Canyon Dam, on the border between Utah and Arizona, was built in 1963 to harness the Colorado River for the production of electrical energy. The dam created Lake Powell, a great man-made body of water.

In the middle of these extremes, at the very edge of Lake Powell, lie Monument Valley and Glen Canyon. Although this area receives only 4 to 8 inches of precipitation a year, its canyons were carved by erosion by water. The area is a meeting place for the most important tributaries of the stretch of the Colorado River that flows through Utah and is not limited to arid or semiarid zones. Piñon pines and junipers cover just as much area as that colonized by shrubs and bushes typical of desert vegetation.

The plateau gives southern Utah and its canyon country a unique appearance. Fractures in the earth's surface, differences in altitude and climate, and the structure of the rocks have made this land different from the surrounding geography. The greatest difference in scenery and habitat can be seen in the southwestern corner of the state, a boundary that divides the Colorado Plateau from the Basin and Range Province, the great desert basin crowned by the Great Salt Lake. In just over 180 miles the land changes from the lowest point in Utah, Beaver Wash Dam, with a desert climate, to an altitude of 6,900 feet on the juniper- and piñon-covered slopes of Capitol Reef.

Between these two points is the Great Staircase, an impressive sequence of enormous rock steps that lead from the Grand Canyon to the heart of the Colorado Plateau in Utah. The earth rises from 4,495 feet to over 16,405 feet, in a series of magnificent, colorful vertical walls that encompass 200 million years in geological time. The lowest and most ancient point is Vermilion Cliffs. The next step is White Cliffs, dating back to the Jurassic period (204–130 million years ago) and sculpted in sandstone, the same stone found in Zion, Capitol Reef, and Canyonlands national parks, the cliffs of Lake Powell, and the rocky formations of Dead Horse Point. Gray Cliffs are formed of gray schist, which solidified around the end of the Cretaceous period (130–65 million years ago), when most of Utah was still under water. Most visitors to this area begin their trip at Pink Cliffs and end their visits in Bryce Canyon National Park and Cedar Breaks National Monument.

86–87 *The red walls of Glen Canyon, carved by the Colorado River over the course of millions of years, are submerged under the dark waters of Lake Powell.*

Petrified Forest and Monument Valley are rainbows of color petrified in wood and a spectacular sight. Petrified Forest National Park preserves a remote and fascinating past. It seems hard to imagine that the enormous plateaus of Arizona were once the site of an enormous equatorial forest. About 225 million years ago, in the Triassic period, the continents were fused into a single supercontinent called Pangea, and the Petrified Forest was one of many forests growing in a marshy basin near the Equator. Ferns and moss surrounded now-extinct tall trees that covered the territory, where dinosaurs roamed.

Everything has changed since then: The continents have drifted throughout the asthenosphere, and all that remains of ancient Pangea is geological evidence such as the wide crescent of west Africa that perfectly matches the convex borders of eastern Latin America. As continental drift moved the land farther and farther north, the giant fallen trees piled up in the still waters of the swamps, where they were covered by sediments, mud, and ash produced by frequent volcanic eruptions in the region.

The Petrified Forest also contains an enormous variety of fossils. Fossils of fish from the Triassic period have been discovered, with two varieties of shark and the remains of numerous reptiles and dinosaurs, including a phitosaurus, a reptile similar to a crocodile, which reached a length of 32 feet.

But the Petrified Forest's charm is not the glimpse of a calendar too old to comprehend or the extraordinary chemical and physical processes that are the joy of enthusiastic paleontologists, but rather the colors, shadows, tones, and forms that give life to this natural sculpture, a unique spectacle that has no equal anywhere else in the world.

91 right
The rocky, vertical walls of the mesas, plateaus squared off by natural forces, are silhouetted against the endless sky. These wild lands were once inhabited by Navajos and traveled by occasional solitary cowboys. The entire Valley of the Gods region borders the Navajo reservation.

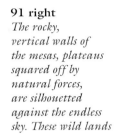

90 *The Valley of the Gods is a vast expanse of red land broken by rocky pinnacles and walls. This deep, 2,142-square-mile valley is on the Utah–Arizona border, not far from the San Juan River region.*

91 left
The Valley of the Gods is popular with visitors, who follow Highway 261 to Monument Valley. This scenic road offers a view of many natural architectural masterpieces.

92 top
The Anasazi built small dams to contain and channel the sudden torrents of water that ran through their land, inundating it for brief periods after the rains. The Anasazi of Monument Valley were able to cultivate small patches of land along the banks of the channels they built, irrigating their fields of corn, beans, and squash. The first inhabitants of these lands left behind hundreds of small settlements. Anasazi communities were usually small and intimate, situated in isolated canyons, and constructed inside natural caverns on the walls of the gorge. Today, some of the few remaining traces of this civilization include the petroglyphs on the walls of numerous caves.

Monument Valley is often called the eighth wonder of the world. Its rock spires that reach up to the sky, the massive rectangular shapes incongruously forgotten by erosion, and the pinnacles of pink sandstone induce reverence and respect in almost every visitor. It is no coincidence that the region, in the heart of the Navajo reservation, is known the world over and immortalized in photographs that attempt to capture the spectacular effects of dawn and dusk, which in this area seem to take on unique tones of light and color. It takes a great leap of imagination to comprehend that once, millions of years ago, Monument Valley was a solid plateau as high as the monumental remains visitors admire today.

The area's stark landscape sets off rock sculptures carved by nature over the millennia. Today, only a few Navajo shepherds manage to eke out a living here, with great effort that affords little profit. But at one time, hundreds of Anasazi lived in this area, after they successfully resolved the problem of chronic lack of water.

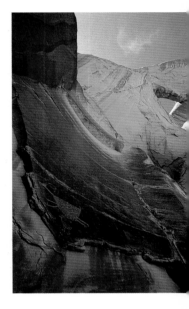

92–93 The warm light of sunset embraces the majestic rocks of the Navajo reservation, a land made famous by the Hollywood film industry.

93 The effects of more than 25 million years of wind and water have transformed an immense plateau into one of the greatest marvels on the face of the Earth: Monument Valley.

94 right
*Immutable and
immobile sentinels,
the rock cathedrals of
Monument Valley
were impassive
witnesses to Kit
Carson as he hunted
bands of Navajo
and, later,
to the chases and
unforgettable rides
of John Wayne.*

95 *The red rock that
characterizes
Monument Valley is
transformed by
atmospheric agents
and undergoes great
changes every day as
the light varies: fiery
red at dawn and
dusk, okra yellow at
midday, and ghostly
black at night.*

94 left
*Vertical pinnacles
that seem
to defy every law
of gravity and
shimmering,
brilliant red walls
characterize the
immense spaces of
Monument Valley.
Even the names*

*attributed to these
rock formations
emphasize the curious
forms that time and
atmospheric agents
have created: Castle
Rock, Totem Pole,
Three Sisters, and Big
Chief are only a few.*

96 *John Ford discovered these vast lands and brought them to popular attention in 1939, making them famous tourist* *attractions. The American director shot seven films in Monument Valley, the first of which was* Red Cloud.

97 *Monument Valley typifies the legendary West: It has the bold curves of Navajo country, the aridity of the vast land, the great cloudless skies, the imposing fire-red* *monoliths, the vast stretches of sand, the thorny shrubs, the wild and narrow canyons, the labyrinth-like gorges, and the cathedrals of stone.*

98 bottom
The desert, always considered synonymous with lifelessness and desolation, is full of surprises. The petroglyphs on this rock in Saguaro National Park testify to the presence of humans in this area in the distant past.

98–99 *It is said that the desert is indifferent to life or death. Here there is no leafy shelter and no shady refuge, only the skull of a coyote and the sun-bleached bones of some four-legged creature.*

98 top
Cactus are often used as symbols of the arid desert. These plants have developed every possible strategy to best survive the scorching temperatures, from the thorns on their skin to their specially adapted root systems.

The Southwest's landscapes are changeable and unpredictable. The Sonoran Desert that runs from Arizona to New Mexico is unforgiving. Every summer in villages along the border, the U.S. Border Patrol and the Mexican government post signs that read: "Dangerous desert. Lack of water and high temperatures in the desert can cause death. For your own safety, do not attempt to cross." The United States is less than 124 miles away, an enticing opportunity for the people who entrust their lives and a thousand dollars to the so-called coyotes, or Mexican guides, who guarantee a clandestine passage to the promised land of North America.

But although the desert is a harsh place, it is also an ode to life. Plants and animals live and grow here. If a handful of sediment collects in any fissure between the rocks, a plant will sprout immediately. The same holds for the communities of animals that have adapted to the desert's extreme conditions, including the coyote, the javelina (a pig-like creature with a large head and short legs), and the lizards, snakes, scorpions, and insects that make up the teeming desert ecosystem.

The Colorado Plateau extends north and east of Flagstaff and includes parts of the Great Basin Desert, with a finger in Arizona that is often called the Painted Desert. It is a strange, complex, enchanted place, with geology as bizarre as the biodiversity of the Sonoran Desert is great. The whole area is dotted with canyons, horizons against which colossal blocks of rock stand out, with broad, windswept plateaus. The interior of the Mojave Desert in the northwestern corner of the Grand Canyon State is the most arid and inhospitable desert on the North

The Painted Desert is a strange and fantastic part of Arizona, an expanse of hills and plateaus tinged with incredible colors.

American continent. An average of only 5 inches of rain a year falls on Lake Havasu, a man-made lake in Arizona. This minuscule amount of rainfall is enough to support plants, such as the chaparral, or creosote bush, which can live more than 10,000 years and are the oldest living things on the planet. This is also the land of the Joshua tree, a type of yucca that has become a symbol of the Mojave Desert.

The Chihuahuan Desert is located almost diametrically opposite the Sonoran, in the southeast corner of Arizona, on the border of Mexico and New Mexico. This desert is probably the least familiar of the deserts in the area, and it has two natural areas that are essentially unknown to tourists: The first is Texas Canyon, a mountain range made almost entirely of rocks; and the second is Wilcox Playa. From a distance, the latter looks like a large lake shimmering on the horizon, but it is only a mirage, although this 50-square-mile imaginary body of water was a lake at one time. Absolutely nothing seems to grow in this area, but here, too, in one of the most arid and ungenerous places on earth, life exists in abundance.

About 15 miles southwest of Alamogordo, in New Mexico, is White Sands National Monument, 230 square miles of white dunes, with grains that look like ocean sand but are actually tiny particles of eroded rock. The rock dates from the Permian period (280 million years ago) when it could be found in the the Sacramento and San Andreas mountains. The mountains were made of sedimentary rock, sandstone, and limestone and eroded

over the course of the millennia, and although the smaller particles were washed away by the rain, the crystals of limestone, calcinated and dried by the sun, began to pile up toward the northeast, pushed by the prevailing southwesterly winds. Today, the particles have accumulated to become the continuously shifting, dazzling dunes of White Sands National Monument. At first sight, it is difficult to tell if the dunes are made of sand or snow. Dunes Drive, a 16-mile route that can be followed by car, provides an introduction to the history of White Sands. Parking areas are set up along the route to permit visitors to explore these snow-white dunes on foot as well. But keep in mind that digging in the dunes can be dangerous: The sand is extremely unstable and can collapse suddenly, suffocating anyone below. The warnings don't bother the sand-surfers, who surf the sand on a board as if it were water or snow. The sport is not prohibited, but it must be practiced away from the road. From May to September, when there is a full moon, don't miss the chance of taking a walk along the dunes, when White Sands glows in the cold light of the moon.

102 *Isolated trees defy the fine sand of White Sands National Monument in New Mexico. The park contains about 230 square miles of almost exclusively of dunes of fine, snow-white "sand."*

**102–103
and 103 top**
*The tiny particles
that make up the
vast expanse of White
Sands National
Monument are not
grains of sand but the
result of the erosion of
the Sacramento
Mountains and
the San Andreas
Mountains about 280
million years ago.*

Plants that live in desert regions survive by adapting to the scarcity of water. Cactus leaves, for example, are little more than spines to reduce the surface area exposed to the sun, and the plant's "skin" is thick, resembling leather, to reduce evaporation and transpiration and retain as much water as possible. The plant's root system may be ample and shallow to intercept and store all water and moisture available, or it may reach deep into the earth in search of natural reserves hidden under the sunbaked surface.

Animals that live and reproduce in the southern area of the Southwest have adapted to the particular climate of the territory. Mammals, for example, customarily avoid sunlight and are most active in the evening and nighttime hours. Some rodents that are permanent residents of the desert do not drink water but metabolize it from certain seeds they consume. Reptiles are most adapted to the extreme conditions. The area has poisonous snakes, including a variety of rattlesnakes, but, despite their terrible reputation, these reptiles prefer to flee rather than attack. But it is certainly safer to observe the great variety of lizards that live in the desert quietly and from a distance.

106–107 *The light of dawn creates a mirage-like reflection across the vast expanse of the Great Salt Lake.*

107 *The Great Salt Lake is not only a vast arid zone used as a landing area for returning spaceships,*

it is also a mineral deposit with great potential, a natural reservoir for future generations.

The Southwest's Great Salt Lake is so big it has been mistaken for the Pacific Ocean. Imaginative geographers called it "the American Dead Sea," but geologists know that the lake is the remains of Lake Bonneville, an ancient giant that covered an area 52 square miles in size.

In the past, experts in applied engineering saw Great Salt Lake as an obstacle to be overcome and a potential threat to human activity; the mining industry saw it as a reservoir full of easily extractable wealth; and tourists considered it a must-see attraction.

108 top
A majestic elk in Rocky Mountain National Park, a vast territory that became a park in 1915.

108 bottom
The flat mesas of New Mexico are a geographical prelude to the sharp peaks of the Colorado mountains, an alpine area of incalculable value.

108–109 and 109 top
The first white Americans entered the Rocky Mountain region in 1806. Twenty-seven-year-old lieutenant Montgomery Pike left Fort Belle Fontaine, north of St. Louis, on July 15, 1806, to explore the regions to the southwest of the immense new territory of the Louisiana Purchase, bought from Napoléon in 1803 for $15 million. On November 15, Pike saw the Rocky Mountains, at that time known as the Mexican Mountains, for the first time. From the plain, he saw an imposing peak similar to "a small blue cloud," as he wrote in his expedition diary. Pike decided to climb the remote peak. Days and days passed, but the mountain never seemed to grow any nearer. In the end, the lieutenant never succeeded in climbing the mountain, but he was the first American to describe the Colorado Rockies in an official report.

Utah is a wonderful place for skiing. The snow is so good that Salt Lake City will host the Winter Olympic Games in 2002. But Utah also has salt flats, woods, mountain lakes, the Great Salt Lake, pine and fir trees, desert lands on the Nevada border, and turbulent rivers. Two major mountain ranges dominate and characterize Utah. To the west is Wasatch Plateau, a sullen mountain range that runs along the entire length of Utah from north to south, a spine of rock that practically divides the state in two, with a crest that soars up to heights of 9,800 to 10,800 feet above sea level. Utah's second mountain range is the Uinta

Mountains, which stretch along 148 miles and are 6 to 10 miles wide.

Violent tectonic activity created the mountainous regions wedged into Utah, Idaho, and Colorado, a patch of territory that hides a troubled past. In the Mesozoic era, 245–265 million years ago, in northeast Utah, the foundations were laid for a series of biochemical processes that would make the area famous in the world of paleontology. For about 120 million years, more than 5,000 species of dinosaurs roamed the planet. The apex of this festival of lizard-like monsters was reached during the Jurassic period, between 204 and 130 million years ago. During that period, the region where winter-sports enthusiasts now swarm was a group of tropical swamps and shallow lakes where life-and-death struggles were played out on a daily basis. The stars of this ruthless battle, both winners and losers, ended up buried in the swamps, where their remains were preserved. Dinosaur National Monument, a protected area crossed by the Green River near Vernal and Cleveland-Lloyd Quarry south of Price, has provided universities and museums all over the world with more dinosaur remains than any other site yet discovered.

The Rocky Mountains offer panoramas, seasons, and sensations and emotions that touch the soul and remain forever in the mind and heart. When the season changes from

110 top and 111
Colorado's Rocky Mountains were famous during the period of the great pioneer caravans, which headed toward the legendary West. The mountains were a formidable

geographical signpost for the pioneers from East. For the men and women of the United States, they signaled the beginning of adventurous life, which has continued to this day.

110–111 *Winter in the heart of the Rocky Mountains can be a harsh experience, as trappers, gold seekers, adventurers, and mountain men discovered when their lust for wealth attracted them to this region. But even this season, whipped by*

blizzards, arctic temperatures, and glacial winds, has its charm. The extreme temperatures are mitigated by the thin, dry air of the high mountains, and when the sky clears and the clouds begin to part, the peaks are a majestic spectacle.

summer to fall, the aspens change color from bright red to a golden yellow in waves that cover the slopes and mountain fields. Indian summer usually arrives unexpectedly between the end of August and October. Flocks of migrating birds fill the sky, warning of the onset of winter, with its thick cloak of snow, under which the trees, meadows, flowers, streams, and mountain lakes hibernate. The Shining Mountains, as the Indians called them, are a distinctive part of the American West, an almost uninterrupted succession of enormous mountains that gaze toward the Pacific and cross Canada, Montana, Idaho, Wyoming, Utah, Colorado, and New Mexico, leaving their last marks in the Earth's crust as far south as Mexico. The southern Rocky Mountains, which are primarily in

Colorado, are divided into about 50 mountains ranges and myriad isolated peaks, from the Elkhead Mountains, the Rawahs, and Park Range in the north, to the Culebra Range that crosses the border of New Mexico. But the most well-known symbol is the mountains of Front Range, the easternmost part of the Rockies, the first range that challenged settlers coming from the East.

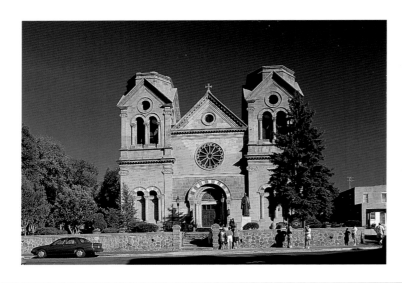

112 top left
The first cathedral of Saint Francis was destroyed in 1680 during the Pueblo revolt. Between 1869 and 1886, it was rebuilt under the direction of the French archbishop Jean-Baptiste Lamy.

112 top right
The Loretto Chapel, inspired by the Sainte Chapelle of Paris, was completed in 1870.

112–113 *The Museum of Indian Art and Culture opened in 1986 and contains a wealth of Indian objects, including a precious collection of pottery.*

113 top
The San Miguel Mission of Santa Fe is the oldest church in New Mexico.

113 bottom
The Fine Arts Museum of Santa Fe was built in 1917 and draws its inspiration from adobe houses.

The cities of the American Southwest are distinguished by often unique histories, traditions, and cultures.

Santa Fe's 55,000 inhabitants love their city, as do the resident artists, photographers, painters, sculptors, writers, and movie stars. Here, where the desert plateaus merge with the Rocky Mountains, the capital of New Mexico straddles the 17th and the 21st centuries and juggles Indian and Spanish cultures with the ever-increasing flow of visitors attracted by the city's unmistakable charm.

Nestled on the slopes of the Sangre de Cristo Mountains, at an altitutde of more than 6,560 feet, Santa Fe has a seductive appearance. The city center, carefully preserved and protected, maintains a stronghold of houses built using ancient local techniques. When the United States took over Mexican administration in 1846, trade with the East Coast increased, and new materials began to change the face of the city's buildings. In its first two centuries of existence, Santa Fe's buildings were only one or two stories high and constructed of adobe.

The city's Territorial style imposed brick facades and decorated roofs. But the flat roofs and low height of the buildings remained, and the city retained its character, becoming an ideal place for an active artistic community.

Santa Fe can become an enchanting snare, a place of hidden delights, with an irresistible call that touches deep and secret places in the soul. It captivated both D.H. Lawrence and Georgia O'Keefe.

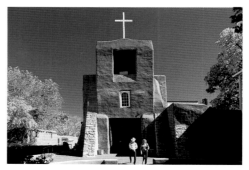

114 top left
The pueblo of Taos, better known as San Geronimo de Taos, is the most evocative of the 19 pueblos in New Mexico. The photograph shows the new pueblo church; the original was destroyed by the U.S. Army in 1847.

114 bottom left
The evocative cemetery of the Taos pueblo is located behind the old mission church and is reserved for Indians who have converted to Christianity.

114 right
A bright blue sky dominates the symmetrical structures of the Taos pueblo. The houses have a particular multilevel form, and the buildings' ovens are in the foreground.

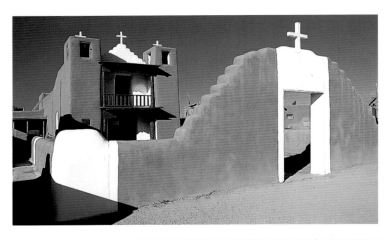

T aos, a little town of 5,000 inhabitants, is easy to love. Perched on the western flank of the Sangre de Cristo Mountains at 6,900 feet above sea level, it preserves a pueblo more than 700 years old and an extraordinary blend of Native American, Spanish, and Anglo-Saxon cultures. Taos has a diverse artistic community, and as in the old Spanish and Mexican towns, life in the city revolves around the plaza, and the surrounding areas offer recreational activities, from skiing to rafting and hiking to bicycling. In summer, Taos is one of the most popular attractions in the Southwest and is assaulted by hordes of tourists. The visitors create quite a disturbance for the colony of painters, sculptors, and writers who have made Taos a refuge and oasis of creativity.

114–115 *The Taos Plaza, now a meeting place for residents and the numerous visitors who come to this part of New Mexico, was fortified to protect the city during the bloody Pueblo revolt of 1680 that drove the Spanish from New Mexico.*

115 top
These images show various buildings in Taos, built with traditional adobe techniques, using a mixture of earth, sand, and clay. Houses built in this manner were known as adobe houses, and the style was generally referred to as Territorial.

ALBUQUERQUE: NEW MEXICO'S NEW METROPOLIS

116 top
Albuquerque was originally a pueblo. In 1350, a group of Tiwa Indians settled this area, and Spanish settlers arrived in 1632. The photographs show two views of the modern city: To the left is Central Avenue, the legendary Route 66, while to the right is a traditional building in the Old Town.

116–117
Albuquerque was founded in 1706, and immediately thereafter a church was erected on the west side of the plaza. This church collapsed, and in 1793 the church of San Felipe de Neri was erected in its place. The two bell towers were added in 1855 and 1856.

*I*t started with a lie and nearly ended with a flood. In the past, Albuquerque was little more than a dusty outpost on the northern fringe of the Spanish colonial empire in America, a small, rustic village of fortified adobe houses along the banks of the Rio Grande. Today, Albuquerque is the largest and most active city in New Mexico, a great metropolis that stretches 12 miles east of the river, to the slopes of the Sandia Mountains and to Cibola National Forest, and continues 4 miles west to a jagged volcanic escarpment. Five hundred thousand inhabitants make up this economic heart of the state, a melting pot where New Mexican, Native American, Spanish, and Anglo-Saxon cultures have merged.

In 1706, Francisco Cuervo y Valdés, the governor of New Mexico, decided to found a city. He wrote to the viceroy of New Spain, the duke of Alburquerque, and boasted of a flourishing settlement, a great church, and more than 30 families, the minimum required by the colonial Spanish authorities in America to be officially recognized as a town. In reality, there were not 15 families, but the astute governor was careful to tickle the duke's vanity by discretely noting that the new city would be named after him. And so it was, although, in the early 1800s the first "r" in the princely name was dropped. Valdés's little white lie permitted the village to grow until it became a mandatory stop on El Camino Real between Mexico and Santa Fe.

Today, Albuquerque is a modern city, and a drive on the Interstate highways, which divide the city into four parts with interlinked junctions and underpasses, feels like driving in a sprawling California-style metropolis. Unfortunately, many people who visit Albuquerque never go beyond the outer shell of the city. Beyond its new downtown area, its convention centers, the financial district that, like any respectable American financial district, flaunts the bold lines of its glass skyscrapers, luxury hotels, and underground shopping malls, there is a discreet and hidden charm to Albuquerque that can only be discovered a little at a time. Explore it, and you will realize that this old Spanish colonial outpost is closer to Texas than to California, more in step with adobe houses than with skyscrapers, more rooted in Native and Spanish than Anglo-Saxon culture.

117 top
Every year Albuquerque hosts an international hot-air balloon festival, when New Mexico's endless are dotted with innumerable spots of color.

117 bottom
Even recently constructed buildings reflect the classical architectural style of the pueblo, a style known as Spanish Colonial or Pueblo Revival.

**118 top
and 119 top**
*Not far from
Albuquerque is
Laguna Pueblo.
The pueblo is actually
a group of six villages
built by settlers who
were fleeing the
atrocities and
destruction of
the Spanish as they
attempted to
reconquer New
Mexico. The
photograph to the left
shows the white adobe
walls of the San José
Mission.*

118 center
*The Saint Augustine
Mission, completed in
1720, stands in the
pueblo of Isleta.
Father Juan de
Padilla, one of the two
priests who
accompanied
Coronado during his
expedition in search
of the legendary cities
of Cibola, is buried
under the church's
altar.*

118 bottom
*Ladders in the Acoma
pueblo point up to the
wide blue sky. The
original settlement,
which may date from
the 7th century,
witnessed the arrival
of troops following
Coronado's expedition
in 1540.*

118–119 *The pueblo of Acoma is a magical place known as Sky City, because it is on top of a high mesa that overlooks an extraordinary panorama.*

DENVER, THE MILE-HIGH CITY

Denver must contend with an ambiguous, somewhat irreverent, and fundamentally erroneous image. For some, Denver is only an overgrown, rough cow town, while for others it's a mandatory stop on any trip to the Southwest.

Denver's Larimer Street is one of the most elegant districts in the capital of Colorado. Much water has passed under the bridge since Jack Kerouac, a writer who became one of the most authoritative interpreters of the Beat generation, described his first encounter with Denver in the pages of *On the Road*. Larimer Street is no longer the scene of the raids Kerouac described. The symbol of the city's break with its rough past is Denver International Airport, which opened in 1995. It has 84 gates to serve an annual traffic of 34 million passengers, covers an area twice as large as Manhattan, and is the largest commercial port on the planet.

Perched on the slopes of the towering Rocky Mountains, Denver lies on the far western tip of the Great Plains of North America and shares the reality of the two worlds it reflects. The city is the administrative, financial, and commercial center of the state. It has 2 million inhabitants, all of whom are accustomed to breathing the crystalline air 5,278 feet above sea level. Visitors discover unexpected things in Denver: The city was, after all, a livestock center and home to cowboys. For a few weeks in January, the city relives its past when it hosts the National Western Stock Show and Rodeo, an enormous livestock fair accompanied by the most important and famous rodeo in the world. But the rodeo era has been overshadowed by the age of technology, and the activities that were once carried out during the fairs are now, for the most part, automated.

120 left
Denver has enormous potential. Thirty-five percent of its residents are between 18 and 35 years old.

120 top right
Denver is the largest metropolis in the Rocky Mountain region. The city's skyscrapers host a workforce that is among the most educated in the United States, with a percentage of college graduates second only to Washington, DC.

120–121 *Denver never fails to astonish: Around the city are a large number of parks, and the city center has the most well-organized network of urban paths in the country. The city also has the largest sporting goods store in the world.*

121 top
Denver has an average of 300 days of sun a year, more than San Diego or Miami.

122 top
Threatening clouds darken the sky and frame the low houses of Estes Park.

122–123 *Almost unchanged from a century ago, Durango is a point of departure for trips into the Rocky Mountains.*

123 top and center
Whimsical names with old-fashioned charm appear on the buildings of the traditional houses in Silverton, a mining town at the foot of the Rocky Mountains. The gold rush of the last century brought innumerable adventurers in search of fortune to these territories. Today, the new adventurers are tourists, and, in particular, winter-sports enthusiasts.

123 bottom
Trinidad stands on the old site of El Rio de las Animas Perdidas en Purgatorio, one of the most important stopover areas on the Santa Fe Trail. Settlers stopped here at the foot of the great mountains as they prepared to face the long and perilous crossing.

124 left

Darrel Duppa, an adventurous Englishman and one of the first farmers in this harsh area, made an erudite prediction that would give Phoenix its name. Duppa was convinced that a new city would rise from the ashes of the Hohokam civilization, just as the mythical phoenix rises from its own ashes every 500 years. The top photograph shows one of the traditional houses that line Heritage Square; bottom is one of the numerous churches that characterize the capital of Arizona.

Phoenix was founded in 1870, and because wood was scarce, buildings were constructed of adobe, a link with the ancient Hohokam villages of the city's past. Phoenix has been growing at an astounding pace in recent years and has developed from a frontier town in the middle of nowhere to one of the most attractive cities in the United States. Sunny skies, breathtaking desert panoramas, a location in the heart of the historic West, first-class hotels, athletic activities, some of the most important technology centers and offices in the United States, a reasonable cost of living, and a relaxed and casual lifestyle are some of Phoenix's attractions.

Phoenix also has a wonderful climate. The city has more than 300 days of sun and only 7 inches of rain a year. The summer heat can be oppressive in Phoenix, but most of the city is air-conditioned and cool, crisp mountain air is only two hours away by car. Phoenix is at its most captivating in winter. While most of the state is caught in the grip of cold, the capital of Arizona is bathed in sunlight.

Phoenix has a special and sometimes conflictual relationship with its environment, the Sonoran Desert. The state capital and its suburbs are not desert locations. Most importantly, the city has never wanted to be one. Its urban model is a desert oasis. In 1911, the Roosevelt Dam pent up the waters of the Salt River and changed the face of the city. The canals, originally destined only for agricultural use, create a verdant urban panorama.

Golf courses are the most frequent sight in the Valley of the Sun, but other Phoenix attractions include the Scottsdale Mall, one of the most beautiful city parks in the United States, and Fountain Hills, north of the Salt River Indian Reservation, with the highest fountain in the world, a jet of water that shoots 561 feet up. Phoenix is a wonderful place to visit between October and May, when the temperatures are moderate. It has been a famous vacation area since the 1930s when it was a winter holiday resort popular with William Wrigley Jr., the chewing-gum magnate, Cornelius Vanderbilt, Jr,. and Frank Lloyd Wright.

124 right and 125 top *Phoenix was modeled after eastern cities. These photographs show the modern, metropolitan character of the city today.*

124–125 *Eight carefully reconstructed buildings from the 19th century line Heritage Square. Rosson House, shown in the photograph, was built in 1895 and belonged to Ronald Rosson, a doctor in the U.S. Army.*

126 top left
The skyscrapers of central Tucson seem to rise up in defiance of Arizona's endless sky. The city is located in a valley bounded by four mountain ranges: Santa Catalina, Santa Rita, Rincon, and Tucson.

126 top right
The panoramic view shows Tucson's original center, which has now undergone a complete transformation. The "city at the foot of the dark mountain," Chuckson in the Pima Indian language, is familiarly known as Old Pueblo.

126-127 *The Tucson skyline and the Santa Catalina Mountains not far behind seem smothered in fiery clouds.*

TUCSON, THE CITY AT THE
FOOT OF THE DARK MOUNTAIN

T ucson gets its name from the Pima Indian word *chukeson*, which means "at the foot of the dark mountain." Tucson is different from Phoenix in many ways. In Tucson, there is a saying: "They pay you in sunshine." "Old Pueblo," as its inhabitants call it, is not known for high wages. But, with the passing of time, the city has filled with people willing to sacrifice some of their paycheck in exchange for living in a wonderful climate and splendid natural surroundings.

Tucson was founded by the Spanish in 1775 on the foundations of a much older Hohokam settlement. From 1867 to 1877 it served as the territorial capital of Arizona before the capital was permanently transferred to Phoenix. Now, the city stretches into a desert delimited by four mountain ranges located at the four cardinal points and has 700,000 residents.

The Santa Catalina Mountains, a flow of granite and gneiss to the north of the city, are 9,150 feet high, and the softer, more rounded Rincon Mountains rise to the east. The two peaks of the Santa Ritas are often covered with snow, and the peak of Mount Wrightson soars

9,445 feet high. To the west of the city are the low Tucson Mountains. The mountains make Tucson's summers less oppressive than in other cities in southern Arizona.

Unlike the capital, which is always struggling to deny the desert, Tucson has learned to accept it, and perhaps even to love it. This outlook may exist because Tucson has no rivers like Phoenix's Salt River that could be dammed to provide water for large-scale irrigation. The rivers of Tucson are arroyos, dry creeks for most of the year but subject to flash floods during the violent summer thunderstorms.

The symbol of the city is the University of Arizona. In 1885, it was decided to locate the largest university in the state in Tucson. The university opened in 1891, with a single building, six professors, and 36 students. Now, with its 36,000 students, the university adds rhythm and tone to the cultural life of a city that is more cultivated and intellectual than the capital, and much less opulent. Perhaps this is why Old Pueblo has essentially remained a city made to human measure, where one can visit its most interesting points on foot.

127 top
Students at the University of Arizona. The university opened in 1885, and for 20 years thereafter only 10 students graduated each year. Today, more than 36,000 students are enrolled.

127 bottom
This modern metal sculpture stands near the Tucson library, not far from the Pima County Courthouse.

THE SPANISH BAROQUE MISSION OF SAN XAVIER DEL BAC

M ission San Xavier del Bac near Tucson is the site of perhaps the most beautiful Spanish colonial building in the United States. The dazzling white church stands out clearly against the deep blue desert sky, a symbol of the faith of the early Spanish settlers and converted Papago Indians. Also known as "the white dove of the desert," the mission was founded by Father Eusebio Francisco Kino in 1700 and named after the patron saint. The name Bac, a Papago word which means "where the water rises," comes from the name of an Indian village. The mission's present-day structure was built between 1778 and 1797 and blends various architectural styles: Arabic, Byzantine, and Mexican influences can be seen. The artisans succeeded in overcoming many difficulties, including a

lack of materials, and erected a building in a style that is naive yet effective. There was no marble available, so the high altar was painted to simulate marble. The same is true of the majolica tiles and the candleholders, which are frescoed on the wall of the church. A little hill to the east contains a replica of the grotto of Lourdes and has a view of the mission. San Xavier del Bac is still a Catholic church, and mass is held Monday to Saturday at 8:30 a.m., and Sunday at 8 a.m., 9:30 a.m., 11 a.m. and 12:30 p.m.

128–129
Unfortunately, the name of the architect who designed the mission complex is unknown. The original building was built by the Jesuit missionary Eusebio Francisco Kino in 1700 but was destroyed in 1751 during the tumult caused by the Pima Indian rebellion.

SALT LAKE CITY,
THE CAPITAL OF
THE BEEHIVE STATE

Lying in a large valley in the heart of the Rocky Mountains, Salt Lake City is important to understanding the soul of Utah. In the Beehive State, the roots of modernity and progress lie in the land around the gigantic Mormon Temple, the focal point of Salt Lake City. Enormous radio and television stations, the leading newspapers, the most important cultural and athletic events, the international airport, the shopping centers, the administrative and financial centers, the world headquarters of the Church of the Latter-Day Saints, and basically every segment and every essential aspect of modern life can be found in this city. The Temple of the Mormon church overlooks and shapes the city's profile.

When it was founded in 1847, Salt Lake City was intended to be the headquarters for all Latter-Day Saints in the world. The granitic solidity of that state unto itself was immediately challenged by the social ferment that shook the entire United States in those turbulent years. It started in 1849 with the California gold rush. Hordes of forty-niners flowed toward the Pacific coast, often stopping off in Salt Lake City,

a rapidly growing town that offered significant possibilities for development. Then Catholic Irish miners and Jewish German merchants began to arrive, attracted by the wealth that the soil beneath the Beehive State offered, a treasure that Brigham Young had formally prohibited to his followers. In the early 20th century, these immigrants were followed by Italian, Greek, and Slavic workers, and in more recent times, Mexican and Asian laborers.

The arrival of peoples of religions and cultures other than the Mormon faith was not painless. Salt Lake City was divided in two, with an invisible wall separating the northern part from the southern portion. To the north was the Temple, Young's residence, the administrative offices, and the Mormon shops, and to the south was the alternative stronghold, with other buildings constructed by the multifaith community, overlooked by the Salt Lake Stock Exchange and dominated by securities from mining industries. During those years, the magnificent Catholic cathedral, the Capitol, new residential districts and new parks were built, and the city began to take on its present-day appearance.

INDEX

c = caption

A

Acoma Pueblo, 31c, 118c, 119c
Acowitz (Indian chief), 20
Agriculture
    Anasazi agricultural techniques, 22,
        24
    European agricultural practices, 32,
        34
Albuquerque, New Mexico, 117
American flag, 36c
Amphitheaters, 81c
Anasazi Indians
    artifacts, 20c, 22c, 23c, 31c
    culture and civilization, 8, 20, 22,
        24, 28c, 88c
    disappearance of, 24, 26, 30
    settlement in Canyon de Chelly, 76c
    settlement in Monument Valley, 93,
        93c
Animal husbandry, 32
Animals
    coyotes, 98
    desert mammals and reptiles, 104,
        104c
    javelina, 98
    puma, 72c
Apache Indians, 8, 30, 46–47
Aquarius Plateau, 76
Archaeological excavations, 24
Arches National Park, Utah, 62, 62c,
    64c, 66c, 71c
Arizona
    canyons of, 12, 22, 32, 41c, 56c,
        57–58, 59c, 79, 85
    gold discoveries in, 38
    missions in, 34, 129
    Phoenix, 124–125
    Tucson, 11, 34, 36, 127, 129
Arroyos (rivers), 127
Astronomy, 24, 28
Atom bomb, creation of the, 53–55

B

Baskets, Anasazi, 20c, 22, 24
Beaver Wash Dam, 85
Bell Rock, 72
Biaeu, W. J., 35c
Big Chief rock formation, 94c
Bisbee, Arizona, 38
Bonney, William (Billy the Kid), 43c
Book Cliffs, 76

Bryce Amphitheater, 81c
Bryce Canyon National Park, Utah, 12,
    76, 81c, 85
Buena Vista, Battle of, 36c
Buildings
    adobe houses, 113, 113c, 114c
    Anasazi, 20, 24
    Hohokam, 28

C

Calamity Jane, 43c
Canals, 28, 124
Canyon de Chelly, Arizona, 24c, 76,
    76c
Canyonlands National Park, Utah, 22,
    62, 72, 72c, 85
    Island in the Sky area, 26c
Capitol Reef, 62, 76, 85
Carson, Kit, 94c
Cartographers, 32
Castle Rock, 94c
Cathedral Rock, 72, 75c
Caverns, 20
Cedar Breaks National Monument,
    Utah, 85
Central Pacific Railroad, 50, 53
Chaco Canyon, 28c
Chaco civilization, 24
Chaco Culture National Historical
    Park, New Mexico, 24, 28c
Chama River, 34, 35c
Chapultepec, Battle of, 36c
Chihuahuan Desert, 101, 101c
Chinle River, 24c
Christianity, 22, 34, 35c, 114c
Church of San Felipe de Neri, 117c
Church of the Latter-Day Saints
    (Mormons), 48–50, 131, 131c
Churches
    New Mexico, 11c, 34, 113c, 114c,
        117c
    Phoenix, 124c
    Tucson, 129
Cibola National Forest, New Mexico,
    117
Clanton brothers, 42c
Cliff Canyon, 20, 22c
Cliff dwellings, 8, 20c, 24, 24c
Climate
    changes and great drought between
        1276 and 1299, 24, 26
    in Denver, 121c
    in Grand Canyon, 58
    in Phoenix, 124

in Rocky Mountains, 111c
Cochiti Pueblo, 31c
Colorado, 122–123
    Denver, 120–121
    mining, 38, 123c
Colorado Plateau, 30, 62, 62c, 72, 85,
    98
Colorado River, 56c, 57, 57c, 62, 62c,
    84c, 85c
    tributaries, 58, 85
Columbia River, 38c
Columbus, Christopher, 30
Comb Ridge, 76
Conestoga wagons, 48, 48c
Copper mines, 38
Coronado, Francisco Vàsquez de, 32,
    33c, 118c
Cotton, 28
Courthouse rock formation, 72
Cowboys, 40c, 41c
Cretaceous period, 85
Cripple Creek, 11
Crocker, Charles, 53
Crook, Gen. George, 46c
Culebra Range Mountains, 111
Currency, minting, 40c

D

Dead Horse Point, 62, 85
Denver, Colorado, 120–121
Desert, 98c, 99c, 101, 101c
Dinosaur National Monument, Utah,
    108
Dinosaurs, 11, 88
Dunes, 101–102, 102c, 103c, 104c
Duppa, Darrel, 124c

E

Eagle Head rock formation, 72
Earp, Wyatt, 42c
El Rio de las Animas Perdidas en
    Purgatorio, 123c
Elkhead Mountains, 111

F

Farming and irrigation, prehistoric,
    22c
Festivals, 117c
Films
    cowboy life in, 41c
    Monument Valley and the film
        industry, 93c, 94c, 97c

violence and modern-day Western, 38
Fine Arts Museum of Santa Fe, 113c
Flagstaff, Arizona, 22, 98
Foch, Ferdinand, 58c
Ford, John, 97c
Four Corners area, 8, 62
Frank brothers, 42c
Franklin, Missouri, 48
Front Range Mountains, 111
Frontier cities, 38

G

Geronimo, 46–47
Ghost towns, 11c, 38
Glen Canyon, 8c, 62, 85, 85c
Glen Canyon Dam, 8c, 84c
Gold mines, 38c, 39c, 123c
Goldrush of 1849, 38, 131
Grand Canyon, 22, 32, 56c, 57–58, 59c, 85
Grand Canyon National Park, Arizona, 12, 57
Grant, Ulysses S., 50
Gray Cliffs, 85
Great Basin Desert, 98
Great Dunes National Monument, Colorado, 104c
Great Plains, 11, 32, 33c, 48c
Great Salt Lake, 85, 106c, 107
Great Staircase, 85
Green River, 108
Gunnison River, 11

H

Hawikuh Pueblo, 32
Hohokam Indians, 124, 124c, 127
    artifacts, 30c, 31c
    culture and civilization, 28
    disappearance of, 30
Hopi Indians, 24c, 26, 30c, 31c
Horses, 32
Houses, adobe, 113, 113c, 114c

I

Immigration
    immigrant miners, 38, 131
    Mormon, 48, 50, 131, 51c
    railroads and Chinese immigrants, 52c, 53, 53c
    Spanish colonization and European, 34

Independence, Missouri, 48
Irrigation system, prehistoric, 22c, 28c
Isleta Pueblo, 118c

J

James, Frank, 43c
James, Jesse, 43c
Jemez Mountains, 53
Jesuits, 34, 129c
Jurassic period, 11, 85, 108

K

Kachina dolls, 26, 28, 30c
Kaibab National Forest, 57
Kaiparowits Plateau, 76
Kerouac, Jack, 120
Kidder, Alfred V., 22
Kino, Father Eusebio Francisco, 34, 129, 129c
Kiva (religious structures), 24

L

Laguna Pueblo, 118c
Lake Bonneville, 107
Lake Havashu, 101
Lake Mead, 57
Lake Powell, 8c, 57, 84c, 85, 85c
Lamy, Jean-Baptiste, 113c
Landscape
    in Utah, 76
    of western frontier, 8
Lawrence, D. H., 113
Le Sal Mountains, 76
Lead mines, 38
Lexington, Missouri, 48
Limestone, 64c, 102
Lincoln, Abraham, 50
Loretto Chapel, 113c
Los Alamos, New Mexico, 53–55
Louisiana Purchase, 108c

M

McLaury, Thomas, 42c
Manhattan Project, 53–55
Manifest destiny, 44
Map, American Southwest, 12–13
Mason, Charley, 20
Mesa Verde National Park, Colorado, 20, 20c
Mesa Verde plateau, 20
Mesozoic era, 108

Mexico, independence from Spain, 36, 36c
Mill Elrey, battle of, 36c
Mining cities, 38, 123c
Missionaries, 32, 33c, 34
Missions, 34, 113c, 118c, 129
Mojave Desert, 98, 101
Monument Valley, 8c, 12c, 85, 88, 91c, 93
    film industry and, 93c, 94c, 97c
Mormon Church, 48–50, 131
Mormon Temple, 50c, 131, 131c
Mormon Trail, 48, 50, 51c
Mostaert, Jan, 33c
Mother and Child rock formations, 72
Mount Wrightson, 127
Museum of Indian Art and Culture, 113c
Museums, Santa Fe, 113c

N

National monuments
    Colorado, 104c
    New Mexico, 101–102, 102c, 103c
    Utah, 62, 85, 108
National parks
    Arizona, 12, 57, 88, 88c, 98c
    Colorado, 20, 20c, 108c
    Utah, 12, 22, 26c, 62, 62c, 66c, 71c, 72, 72c, 76, 81c, 85
Native Americans, 8, 44c
    Athabaska language group, 30
    extermination of the Indians, 45c
    stagecoach attack by, 44c
    U.S. position toward native peoples, 44–47
Natural Bridge Park, Utah, 75c
Nauvoo, Illinois, 50, 51c
Navajo Indians, 30
    Monument Valley reservation, 93
    Navajo language, 8, 22
    settlement in Canyon de Chelly, 24c, 76c
    Valley of the Gods, 91c
New Mexico. *See also* Pueblos
    Albuquerque, 117
    mesas of, 108c
    missions, 113c, 118c
    Santa Fe, 11, 22, 32, 34, 113
    Spanish colonization in, 31, 34–36
    statehood, 53
New Mexico Territory, 36
Newspaper Rock, 26c
Nizza, Marco da, 33c

O

Oak Creek Canyon, Arizona, 72
OK Corral, 38, 42c
O'Keefe, Georgia, 113
Old Tucson Studios, Arizona, 12
Omaha, Nebraska, 53
On the Road (Kerouac), 120
Oñate, Juan de, 34, 35c
Oppenheimer, J. Robert, 53–55

P

Pacific Railroad, 50
Pacific Railroad Act, 50
Padilla, Father Juan de, 118c
Painted Desert, 98, 99c
Paleontology, 108
Palo Alto, Battle of, 36c
Pangea, 88
Papago Indians, 129
Paria Canyon, Arizona, 79c
Paria Canyon Vermilion Cliff
    Wilderness Area, 79c
Paria River, 79c
Park Range Mountains, 111
Paunsaugunt Plateau, 81c
Peralta, Pedro de, 34
Permian period, 101–102
Petrified Forest National Park, Arizona,
    12, 88, 88c
Petroglyphs, 8, 24, 26c, 28, 93c, 98c
Phoenix, Arizona, 124–125
Pike, Montgomery, 108c
Pima Indians, 28, 34, 127, 127c, 129c
Pink Cliffs, 85
Pinkerton, William, 43c
Plant life
    cactus, 12c, 98c, 104
    in Canyonlands National Park, 72c
    chaparral, 101
    creosote bush, 101
    Joshua tree, 101
    saguaro, 101c, 104c
    yucca, 101c
Pottery, Anasazi, 20c, 22, 22c, 24, 31c
Prehistoric civilizations. *See* Anasazi
    Indians; Hohokam Indians
Promontory, Utah, 50, 52c, 53
Pueblo Bonito, 28c
Pueblo Indians, 24c, 26, 28, 30c
Pueblo revolt of 1680, 113c, 114c
Pueblos
    Acoma Pueblo, 31c, 118c, 119c
    Anasazi villages, 22, 24, 28c

architectural style of, 117c
    Cochiti Pueblo, 31c
    Hawikuh Pueblo, 32
    Isleta Pueblo, 118c
    Laguna Pueblo, 118c
    Pueblo di Taos, 12
    Pueblo Revival style, 117c
    San Ildefonso Pueblo, 11c
    Taos Pueblo, 11c, 12, 114
    Zuni pueblo, 33c

R

Railroads, 50, 52–53
Rainbow Bridge, Utah, 62
Rawahs Mountains, 111
Red Cloud (film), 97c
Religion
    ancient religious structures, 24
    Christianity, 22, 34, 35c, 114c
    Church of the Latter-Day Saints
        (Mormons), 48–50, 131, 131c
Reptiles, 88, 104
Rincon Mountains, 127, 127c
Rio Grande, 12, 32, 34, 35c, 117
Rio Grande Valley, 35c, 53
Roads, Anasazi road system, 24
Rock carvings, 28
Rock formations, 12c, 72, 75c, 94c
Rock sculptures, 11, 62
Rock steps, 85
Rocks
    in Arches National Park, 64c
    in Canyon de Chelly, 76
    in Canyonlands National Park, 26c,
        72c
    in Grand Canyon, 57, 58, 58c, 59c
    in Monument Valley, 94c
    in Sedona, Arizona, 75c
    in White Sands National
        Monument, 101–102, 103c
Rocky Mountain National Park,
    Colorado, 108c
Rocky Mountains, 11, 108, 108c, 111,
    111c, 113, 120
Rodeo, 120
Roosevelt Dam, 124
Roosevelt, Theodore, 8c
Rosson, Ronald, 125c
Route 66, 117c
Royal City of the Holy Faith of Saint
    Francis of Assisi, 34

S

Sacramento, California, 50, 53
Sacramento Mountains, 101–102,
    103c
Saguaro National Park, Arizona, 98c
Saint Augustine Mission, 118c
Saint Francis of Assisi, 34, 113c
Saint Jerome, 47
Salado Indians, 20c
Saloons, 38, 40c
Salt Lake City, Utah, 11, 130–131
    bank in, 40c
    end of Mormon Trail, 50
    Mormon Temple, 50c, 131, 131c
    Winter Olympic Games in 2002,
        108
Salt Lake Valley, 50, 51c
Salt River, 28, 124
Salt River Indian Reservation, 124
San Andreas Mountains, 101–102,
    103c
San Gabriel, 34, 35c
San Geronimo de Taos, 114
San Ildefonso Pueblo, 11c, 31c
San José Mission, 118c
San Juan River, 76, 91c
San Miguel Mission of Santa Fe, 113c
San Rafael Swell, 76
San Xavier del Bac Mission, 34, 129
Sand dunes, 101–102, 102c, 103c,
    104c
Sandia Mountains, 117
Sandstone, 62, 62c, 66c, 85, 102
Sangre de Cristo Mountains, 113, 114
Santa Catalina Mountains, 127, 127c
Santa Fe, New Mexico, 11, 22, 32, 34,
    113
Santa Fe Trail, 48, 49c, 123c
Santa Ritas Mountains, 127, 127c
Sedona, Arizona, 72, 75c
Seven Cities of Cibola, 33c, 118c
Silver mines, 38
Smith, Hiram, 49
Smith, Joseph, 49, 50c, 131c
Snakes, 104
Snaketown, Arizona, 31c
Sonora, New Mexico, 46c
Sonoran Desert, 11, 12c, 98, 101c,
    124
Spanish Colonial style, 117, 117c
Spanish colonization, 31–35, 88c, 117
    independence from Spain, 36, 36c
Spirituality, 24
Stagecoaches, 11c, 43c, 44c

T

Taos Pueblo, 11c, 12, 114
Telegraph, 52c
Texas Canyon, 101
Three Sisters rock formation, 94c
Tiwa Indians, 117c
Tombstone, Arizona, 11, 38, 42c
Totem Pole rock formation, 94c
Train robberies, 43c
Trains, 48
Transcontinental Railroad, 53c
Trappers, 44c, 45c
Treaty of Guadalupe Hidalgo, 36
Triassic period, 88
Tributaries, Colorado River, 58, 85
Trinity Site, 54
Tucson, Arizona, 11, 34, 36, 127, 129
Tucson Mountains, 127, 127c
Twin Nuns rock formations, 72

U

Uinta Mountains, 108
Union Pacific Railroad, 50, 53
University of Arizona, 127, 127c
Utah, 108
    mining, 38
    Mormon Church and creation of,
      48–50
Utes, 20

V

Valdés, Francisco Cuervo y, 117
Valley of the Gods, 91c
Vanderbilt, Cornelius, Jr., 124
Vargas, Diego de, 34, 35c
Veracruz, conquest of, 36c
Verde River, 72
Vermilion Cliffs, 85
Violence, western, 38
Vishnu schist, 58

W

Wagons, covered, 38c, 48, 48c
Wasatch Plateau, 108
Wayne, John, 41c, 94c
West Mitten (rock formation), 12c
Wetherill, Richard, 20
White Cliffs, 85
White Sands National Monument,
    New Mexico, 101–102, 102c, 103c

Wichita Indians, 32
Wilcox Playa, 101
Wright, Frank Lloyd, 124
Wrigley, William, Jr., 124
Wyeth, Newell Convers, 45c

Y

Young, Brigham, 49, 50c, 131
Younger, Bob, 43c
Younger, Cole, 43c

Z

Zion National Park, Utah, 62, 76, 85
Zuni Indians, 32, 33c

136 *Established in 1971, Colorado's Arches National Park has about 2,000 natural arches,* *extraordinary geological phenomena caused by erosion by the wind and rain.*